Literary Anatomies

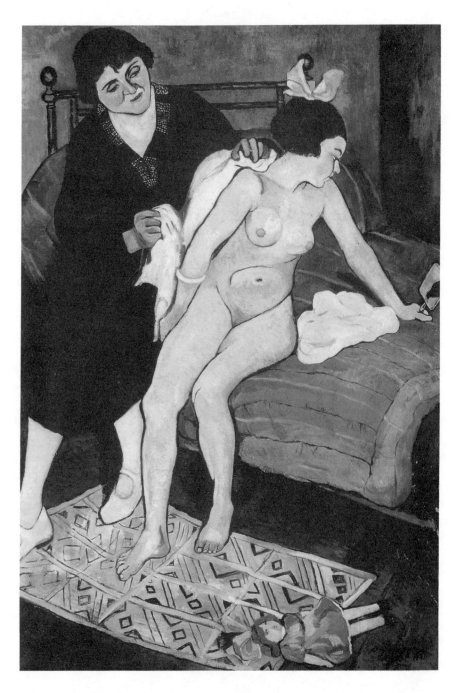

Suzanne Valadon (French, 1865–1938). *The Abandoned Doll*, 1921.
Oil on canvas, 51 × 32 in. The National Museum of Women in the
Arts. Gift of Wallace and Wilhelmina Holladay.

Literary Anatomies

Women's Bodies and Health in Literature

Delese Wear
and
Lois LaCivita Nixon

STATE UNIVERSITY OF NEW YORK PRESS

Cover photo: Suzanne Valadon (French, 1865–1938), *The Abandoned Doll*, 1921. Oil on canvas 51 × 32 in. The National Museum of Women in the Arts. Gift of Wallace and Wilhelmina Holladay.

Chapter 4 originally appeared in *Family Medicine* volume 25 (1993); Chapter 3 in *Women and Health* volume 20 (1993); and parts of Chapter 6 in the *Journal of Women and Aging* 3(4):117–125.

Published by
State University of New York Press, Albany

© 1994 State University of New York

PS
173
·W6
W4
1994

For information, address State University of New York
Press, State University Plaza, Albany, N.Y., 12246

Production by E. Moore
Marketing by Fran Keneston

Library of Congress Cataloging-in-Publication Data
Wear, Delese.
    Literary anatomies : women's bodies and health in literature /
Delese Wear and Lois LaCivita Nixon.
        p. cm.
    Includes bibliographical references and index.
    ISBN 0-7914-1925-8 (HC). — ISBN 0-7914-1926-6 (PB)
    1. American Literature—History and criticism.   2. Women—United
States—Health and hygiene—History.   3. Women and literature-
-United States.   4. Body, Human, in literature.   5. Medicine in
literature.   6. Women in literature.   I. Nixon, Lois LaCivita.
II. Title.
PS173.W6W4   1994
810.9′352042—dc20   93-26096
                                                              CIP

10 9 8 7 6 5 4 3 2 1

For Nancy Seigfreid and Mary Grace Cash Sandler

We have never lived enough. Our experience is, without fiction, too confined and too parochial. Literature extends it, making us reflect and feel about what might otherwise be too distant for feeling.
              —Martha Nussbaum, Love's Knowledge

The institution of medicine has been designed in ways that rein-force sexism, and the effects of medical practice are often bad for women. Most individual medical actions make sense in the context of medicine as it is currently defined, but we need to step back and examine the cumulative effects of some of its practices. We need to see the pattern of medical values and structures as a whole, in or-der to identify patriarchy; only then can we see the sorts of changes that should be made. As long as we focus on the merely personal—that is, on an individual encounter with a particular doctor—we cannot see the systematic force of sexist assumptions in our health care institutions.
              —Susan Sherwin, No Longer Patient

Contents

Acknowledgments

Even though our two names appear on the cover, many others participated meaningfully in the creation of this book. Jeanette Stoffer, Mona Adorni, and Mavis Green were enormously helpful in keeping track of the unwieldy task of permissions correspondence and proofreading drafts. Martin Kohn and Roy Behnke provide a work environment that enthusiastically supports our individual creative efforts. And our editor at SUNY, Priscilla Ross, was always there to provide a gently forthright and thoughtful critique of our work, keeping us hopeful and encouraged that what we were doing was potentially meaningful to others.

Last, because our personal and professional lives are not neatly divisible, we want to acknowledge the nourishing presence of Steve, Ben, and Meredith Broderick; and Jason, Jenn, and Justin Nixon.

Suzanne Valadon (French, 1865–1938). *Nude Doing Her Hair*, 1916. Oil on canvas, 41¼ × 29⅝ in. The National Museum of Women in the Arts. Gift of Wallace and Wilhelmina Holladay.

Introduction

Getting Situated

Because the story of our life
becomes our life

Because each of us tells
the same story
but tells it differently

and none of us tells it
the same way twice
. . . .
and though we listen only
haphazardly, with one ear,
we will begin our story
with the word and
      —Lisel Mueller, from
      "Why We Tell Stories"

Feminist curriculum theorist Patti Lather once wrote a brilliantly convincing essay entitled, "Issues of Validity in Openly Ideological Research: Between a Rock and a Soft Place" (1986). The issues she raised there, as well as in her subsequent writing as a feminist researcher attuned to postmodernism, had to do with the need for theorists and investigators in any domain to acknowledge that interest-free knowledge is impossible; to stop posturing with illusions of objectivity, disinterestedness, and neutrality; and to state upfront their biases and intentions.

1

As the authors of an inquiry into women's health experiences, we too felt the necessity of announcing where we are situated with our intentions for this book, and what we hope will occur as readers study and think about the issues portrayed and discussed here. We intend this book to be a political work, what Hélène Cixous describes as going "beyond the bounds of censorship, reading, the gaze, the masculine command, in that cheeky risk-taking women can get into when they set out into the unknown to look for themselves" (1990, 354). The "unknown" where we venture into women's bodies and medical/health-related experiences can be explored in multiple, conflicting, overlapping, sometimes uncharted spheres of meaning. Here, we brashly move away from (but do not throw away) medical accounts of these experiences, contrasting them with the imaginative forms of poems, short stories, novels, autobiographies—counternarratives often without borders or formulas.

When we read ourselves against a masculinist, medicalized standard, we see ourselves as its effects, its errata. But when we begin to *write* ourselves through our bodies as many of the writers here have attempted, we begin "to render noisy and audible all that [has] been silenced in phallocentric discourse" (Minh-ha 1989, 37). Such writing affirms the fluidity of women's corporeality; generates ways of knowing that may take us beyond ourselves—certainly beyond prescriptive medical narratives; and serves as fertile ground for the construction of collective, always shifting realities. And perhaps many of these counternarratives were written with women's entire bodies, not just their minds and hearts, for "it is a perversion to consider thought the product of one specialized organ, the brain, and feeling, that of the heart" (Minh-ha, 36).

The women's biological, health, or medical issues we examine in these counternarratives are pregnancy and birth (including abortion, adoption, infertility), adolescence, breast cancer, menopause (including hysterectomy), and aging. The politicized feminist current running through it, explicit or implicit in our selections and discussions, may evoke a more reflexive and confrontational reading as it wrecks "partitions, classes and rhetorics, regulations and codes" (Cixous 1976, 886). How might such a reading occur?

When we dive into the emancipatory possibilities evoked by literature, we may be better able to engage in a self-conscious, subversive, ironic philosophical critique of culture, a critique that rejects normative theorizing alleging to describe or prescribe "how it is" or "how it should be" for all women. This rejection includes any attempt to universalize women's experiences—including the forms and degrees of patriarchic oppression—across culture, history, race, and class. These universalizing tendencies have sometimes been the work of feminists themselves, who have tried to locate *the* cause of women's oppression, such as appeals to biology to explain the subjugation of all women.

These tendencies are also reflected in the medicalization of women's health whereby experiences such as birth or menopause become categories or stages all women similarly undergo as they are turned into medically "managed" women. In contrast to such categorical thought, especially that which is grounded in binaries such as good/bad, beautiful/ugly, normal/deviant, we have focused on illusive, dislocative "realities" of literature found in the shadows or in the dark. These realities, once made visible, interrogate the ideological grounding of any universalizing representation of women's biology, health, and medical experiences. Still, biology *is* the very basis for this enterprise, but it is a *volatile* biology, a "mutable intertexture, the stuff that informs our interventions" (Kirby 1991, 14).

As we examine these issues through fiction, contrasting literature with medical accounts, we are not searching for one true story of women's biological, health, and medical experiences to serve as a focus for social criticism and political activism; it is the *variety* of these experiences that may form the basis for such activism. We recognize that this inquiry may lead to questions and problems of essentialism because of our focus on women's biology, but we will not take up that argument here. Rather, we believe that "even if we were to grant that essentialism is unarguably wrong—morally, politically, and logically—we still haven't addressed the ways in which its errors 'work'; how essentialism's scriptures 'come to matter,' how they come to write/right themselves" (Kirby, 10).

Our focus is on the real, material domination of women's bodies in a culture that systematically deploys medicalized, masculinist languages to categorize, abstract, and universalize women's biology. But as Monique Wittig forcefully writes, there is "nothing abstract about the power that science and theories have, to act materially and actually upon our bodies and our minds, even if the discourse that produces it is abstract" (1980, 106).

Still, we emphatically do not deprecate the medical record and the scientific/clinical inquiry that informs it. What we *do* resist is their domination, their crush of other languages, domains, and realms of meaning. Here we put forth fictions and other imaginative narratives to be included in the open-ended texts of women's lived experiences. Adding fictions to explorations of women's health breaks the seal and pops the lid on medicalized, masculinist accounts that "judge, diagnose, digest, name . . . not so much in the sense of the loving precision of poetic naming as in that of the repressive censorship of philosophical nomination/conceptualization" (Cixous 1990, 353).

Engaging in a more sweeping inquiry outside medicine in order to better sense how women may experience biological processes and events, with or without medical intervention, is like a

> tapestry composed of threads of many different hues than one woven in a single color. . . . The theoretical counterpart of a broader, richer, more complex, and multilayered feminist solidarity, the sort of solidarity which is essential for overcoming the oppression of women in its endless variety and monotonous similarity. (Fraser and Nicholson 1990, 35)

Thus, this inquiry seeks to expose the mythical medical and cultural norms that have been perpetuated by those whose interests such standards serve, and internalized too often by women themselves. Our text is narrow in its focus on contemporary North American women and authors; yet even at that, we zealously hope our inquiry is not read as a universalizing attempt to speak for all women within those cultures. Our modest attempt is to begin to unwrap, in one of many possible ways, the medicalized binding of women's bodies.

There is, however, much we do not unwrap here, issues critical to many women in North American culture. We did not, for example, address the multilayered meanings of mental health in a separate chapter. Instead, we attempted to draw these dimensions naturally into other chapters, unable/unwilling to separate the spiritual and emotional dimensions of the body from the biology of the body. Similarly, we did not include a separate chapter on women's sexuality, specifically women loving women. We did so not to ignore lesbian writers/narratives, to imply a heterosexual norm, or to dismiss the oppression of lesbians in our heterosexist culture. Rather, we believed lesbian writers/narratives belonged naturally in each chapter, reflecting a fuller range of women's experiences.

The remainder of this introductory chapter suggests a framework for reading this text, a text that is multivocal with diversity of women's voices describing their own and others' health experiences. We examine the multilayeredness of reading—what readers themselves may bring to a story, and what they may hope to experience or gain as they read, or because they have read. While the interpretive possibilities are multiple—many unknown to us—here we have identified several possible motivations for reading this text, based on our *own* drive to write it, knowing well the unpredictability and untidiness of both writing and reading! We read for knowledge, affirmation, identification, or connection to other women and our health experiences—that is, to construct collective but not universalizable realities; we read to turn ourselves and our thinking upside down, to look at what we have thought about these experiences from different angles. Thus, the reading of this text may be, like the rest of our living, personal *and* political, enabling readers to concretize their own experiences with those in the text, to think about and question how women's biology, health and medical issues are represented, to consider who participates in the construction of this reality, and to unravel whose interests are served within these various constructions.

TAKING IT PERSONALLY

It was in watching them giving birth (to themselves) that I learned to love women, to sense and desire the power and the resources of femininity; to feel astonishment that such immensity can be reabsorbed, covered up, in the ordinary.

—Cixous 1991, 31

"We know ourselves by the stories we tell," wrote the Native American writer Leslie Marmon Silko. Likewise, we begin to know and understand others by the stories *they* tell. In all their various forms, styles, and sounds, stories weave us together as we crisscross with our shared experiences; help us feel connected to others as we live in our various ways the full range of human emotions; and reassure us that others have confronted the same difficulties we face.

Women telling stories to other women have "historic reverberations of the pleasure of women meeting together at the river to wash clothes; in a sewing circle to make a quilt" (Reitz 1991). Listening or reading other women's stories are one important way a woman learns about herself and her body—its magic, its failures, its mysteries.

A good story about a woman's experience is, actually, sometimes like gossip, talk often associated with women that unfortunately is generally perceived as negative. Yet Patricia Spacks, in her splendid book *Gossip,* maintains that serious gossip exists only as a "function of intimacy . . . in a context of trust" (1985,5). Moreover,

> its participants use talk about others to reflect about themselves, to express wonder and uncertainty and locate certainties, to enlarge their knowledge of one another. . . . It provides a resource for the subordinated . . . a crucial means of self-expression, a crucial form of solidarity. (6)

The same could be said of fictions about women, and the unspoken alliances and even fierce attachments readers feel for other women, fictional or otherwise, as they read. This is much like what Deanne Bogdan calls the "poetics of need," a priority of reading for "consolidation of identity, an objective that [makes primary] psychic safety and comfort" (1990, 134).

The poetics of need acknowledges and celebrates that a woman's recognition or validation of her experience in literature can be uplifting. Such literature may act as counter to the daily despair many women experience because of social expectations confining them (disproportionately women of color) "to the kitchens, the caring professions, the service industries and the ranks of the wickedly low-paid or unemployed" (Dunker 1992, 3). Literature can also be a source of complex pleasures and insights, full of messengers who confide in us "though in tongues that are foreign to [us], the secrets of human movements, the news of peoples [we have] never imagined" (Cixous 1991, 55). The fictions found here may reflect what Cixous calls a feminine singular unconscious that is part of a "magic book by more than one author," part of a flesh that has been "superhistoricized, museumized, reorganized, overworked . . . [but] different as one text is from another" (1991, 55–56).

These stories and poems may seize readers' interests because the women's lives and experiences they portray relate to or reveal readers' own lived lives. Compelling fictional lives, found in the private safety of reading, may encourage readers to concretize their own unspoken self-doubt, thus promoting a healing reflexivity when they know they are not alone. These stories, as local genealogies, explain and connect women to other women. Here are affirmations, rituals of belonging, collective self-recovery—all potentially a "balm to wounded spirits" (hooks 1991, 39).

In any act of reading where a reader brings about the convergence of the story with her own beliefs, assumptions, and vulnerability, a meeting takes place where meaning-making occurs. Here, as "the reader passes through the various perspectives offered by the text and relates the different views and patterns to one another, [she] sets the work in motion, and so sets [her]self in motion, too" (Iser 1978, 21).

TAKING IT POLITICALLY

*Insofar as we are taught how to read, what we
engage are not texts but paradigms.*
          —Kolodny 1985, 153

*How does the writing of fiction connect with
shaping a new world? . . . Literature does more
than transmit ideology: it actually creates it.*
          —Dunker 1992, 14

Putting a text in "motion" is our hope that, for some readers, the fictions they read will nourish and provoke them to think about women's bodies, health, and medical issues in a larger, more politicized context. Because fictions emerge from an ambiguous, unsettling, and unstable domain, we believe that reading such fictions can dispel universalizing notions that there are answers, rules, or predictors to how women confront and live through the health and biological events common to many (and in some cases all) women. Just as we have come to recognize that we are constantly moving subjectivities, so are the explanations for women's lived biology, health or medical experiences: one cultural/historical moment after another. Literature can make reality strange by turning around and upside down the familiar and commonplace so that a practice, issue, or object of inquiry portrayed in this or that fiction may resemble only slightly, or not at all, what we knew it to be before.

That is what is found in the following chapters: perhaps a connection, and maybe a disruption of thought, a challenge to what we believe about the events, moments, or issues in women's health. The beliefs readers bring to these experiences are deeply embedded in familial, religious, cultural, or class structures and institutions. And while these are important, often positive connections to others, they can also weight us down, keeping us ashamed, guilty, ignorant, embarrassed, or angry at our bodies over the courses of our lives. Stories can momentarily lift or suspend us above or outside our thinking to examine the limits and boundaries imposed by the structures and institutions that inform us. These stories uncover how women have been bombarded with cues, dictates, admonitions, myths, cautions, advice—the "conventional wisdom" about their bodies, what may or will occur to those bodies, and how they should respond to these occurrences.

Moreover, readers may be lead to examine how much of this conventional wisdom has been further grounded in patriarchic thought. Like Lynne Tillman, "it's certainly on [our] agenda—to challenge the complacent, to question national, familial, racial, and sexual arrangements, to resist structures and institutions that serve the powerful and perpetuate powerlessness" (1991, 99). When we examine normative medicalized accounts of women's bodies and health, or when we read fictions portraying these phenomena, perhaps we can do so as a mode of praxis. The point of feminist criticism, as Patrocinio Schweickart suggests, "is not merely to interpret literature in various ways; the point is to change the world. . . . Literature . . . [is] an important arena of political struggle, a crucial component of the project of interpreting the world in order to change it" (1986, 39).

When we examine women's health and medical experiences in the androcentric discourses of science and medicine, we find discourses that treat women's experiences as analytical categories or stages that can be studied and made known by a rigorous adherence to scientific methods. Thus, it is not our intent to enter in another discourse based on the dualisms of art and science, the immediate and the abstract, feminine specifics and masculine universals. Rather, the literature and discussion found here may illuminate "the relationships between these two worlds—how each shapes and informs the other" (Harding 1988, 288). Or, as Joan Scott asserts, "we need theory that will enable us to articulate alternative ways of thinking about (and thus acting upon) gender without either simply reversing the old hierarchies or confirming them. And we need theory that will be useful and relevant for political practice" (1988, 33).

When we consider what science does not affirm—the world of values, emotions, individual consciousness and lived experience, the particularities of culture and history—we feel an absence, an inattention or dismissal of things quite essential to our dailiness, to the ways we make meaning. Yet when we do try to tell our stories, when we attempt to cull and extract meanings from our own lived experiences, we often interpret our experiences as we have been instructed. Simone de Beauvoir reminds us that "representation of the world, like the world itself, is the work of men; they describe it from their own point of view, which they confuse with the absolute truth" (quoted in MacKinnon 1982, 536). But unlike de Beauvoir, we reject our Otherness as inferior, something to be transcended. Rather, we proclaim the advantages of our Otherness as a "way of being, thinking, and speaking that allows for openness, plurality, diversity, and difference" (Tong 1991, 219). One way to do so is to turn to novels, poems, plays, art, and music, to the "world within which we all live most of our waking and dreaming hours under constant threat of its increasing reorganization by scientific rationality" (Harding, 288).

We read (and need) stories for validation, to find that somehow we are okay and that we are not alone, because others have faced what we have, even if in different ways under unique circumstances. But we also read to find new narratives to replace the old or familiar ones. bell hooks reminds us that readers "cannot approach [a] work assuming that they already possess a language of access, or that the text will mirror realities they already know and understand" (1991, 57). Rather, readers are compelled to deconstruct the way they know by transforming the way they think as the stories interrupt and challenge customary ways of knowing. Feminine writing is, after all, "the very possibility of change, the space that can serve as a springboard for subversive thought, the precursory movement of a transformation of social and cultural standards" (Cixous 1976, 879).

This text is an attempt to reconcile women's needs for solidarity and commonality with pressures for variety and difference. Or as Rosemary Tong puts it, "We need a home in which everyone has a room of her own, but one in which the walls are thin enough to permit a conversation, a community of friends in virtue, and partners in action" (1989, 7).

We begin each chapter and section heading with language from medical, nursing, or other health care professional texts. Our attempt is not, in these short quotations, to portray a universal, generalizable, monolithic position of the medical professions that are filled with high-tech science-babblers who see only disease or female aberrations, never the "soul beneath the bone." We recognize that many from these professions would read such quotations quizzically or critically, finding words that misrepresent their beliefs and practices, or that have little to do with the dailiness of their work. We also recognize that many medical and (especially) nursing texts have dramatically changed over the past several decades by attempting to erase explicit patriarchal, heterosexist, and other biases, most notably in the psychosocial domains. But just as changing pronouns and darkening skins does not make a textbook multicultural, it will take far more than superficial attentiveness to women's lived biology, health, and medical experiences to reduce the masculinist biases of North American medicine.

Our intent, then, is to show that even though health-related issues surrounding women's bodies have been categorized, abstracted, and universalized in the deeply influential domain of medicine, imaginative writing by women about women is another domain from which to think about, to seek understandings, and to honor these lived experiences of women. We do not give equal time to each domain, but offer the clinical epigrams beginning each chapter without comment. The monologic position from which they are extracted has clearly dominated this discourse, and needs no further discussion. Rather, in our attempt to deepen and enlarge the conversation, we fill the pages with women's writing, some unruly, wry, and angry; others thin, weak, and weary. Of course, we did not hear most women's voices, bound as we are by a language and culture in a historical moment. Yet our focus on North American culture does not mean that we dismiss other crucial, often violent practices facing women in other cultures, or even that there is a monolithic North American culture. And we fully acknowledge that our conversation here is not a mirror of the world. But it is still our earnest and ongoing attempt to "bring together scholarship and advocacy in order to generate new ways of knowing that interrupt power imbalances" (Lather 1992, 95).

The remainder of this book, the conversation found here, explores women's bodies, health, biology, and medical experiences portrayed in literature. Chapter 2 examines pregnancy and childbirth, but includes such experiences as abortion, miscarriage, and infertility. Chapter 3 explores girls and young women in their changing bodies. Chapter 4 provides literary accounts of breast cancer, while chapter 5 focuses on menopause. Finally, chapter 6 portrays the various ways women age and think about aging.

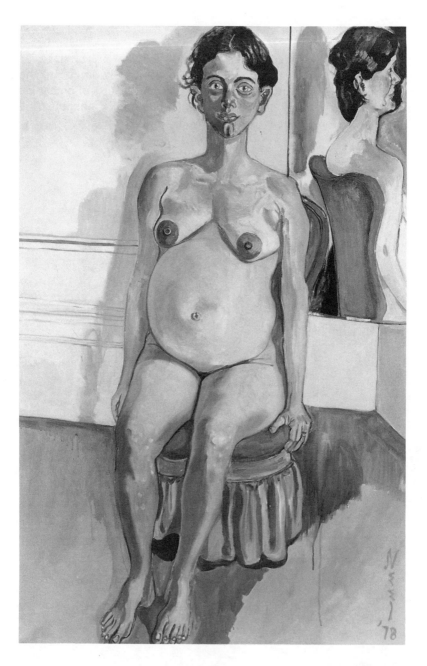

Alice Neel (American, 1900–1984). *Margaret Evans Pregnant*, 1978. Oil on canvas, 57 × 38 in. The Estate of Alice Neel. Courtesy Robert Miller Gallery, New York.

Chapter 1

Pregnancy and Childbirth

Q: What is the rule for carrying the hand under the coverings?
A: The clothes should be properly raised at their lower edges, by the left hand, and then the right hand with the index finger lubricated, passed cautiously up the clothes without uncovering the patient.
—Obstetrical Catechism, 1854

Labor is an acute event terminating the chronic process of pregnancy.
—Fields 1990, 75

Whether fictional or real, pregnancy and childbirth are historicized events. In contemporary North American culture, many women prefer to make choices about how they give birth according to their personal experiences and beliefs about what warrants a healthy, meaningful birth experience, even as they invite informed, caring, appropriate medical intervention. Most women today publicly announce their growing, expansive bellies in every setting imaginable from workplace to beach, and continue to work at jobs until days, even hours, before their deliveries. Many of these women resent the paternalistic intrusions of traditional hospital births, preferring homelike birth centers with more family attention than medical. Many women discuss pregnancy and childbirth explicitly with their partners, children, friends, and colleagues, not restricting such talk to closed-door sessions with their doctors.

Yet all this is a relatively new phenomenon. Until recently pregnancy and childbirth were private matters, restricting not only women's activity and dress, but their very narratives of the experience itself. Prior to the twentieth century, few women published anything, and those who did would have been unlikely to refer explicitly to pregnancy and birth. Privatized writing about these essential but shadowed women's concerns addressed hardships and fears obliquely within prototypically feminine formats—personal writings that were fragmentary and interrupted, a reflection of women's daily uncertainties, responsibilities, and culturally-induced inhibitions. Contemporary readers have discovered how these private genres of writing—diaries, journals, and letters—failed to consider essential physical questions. Instead, they revealed only veiled accounts of pregnancy and birth with little suggestion of physical changes during the nine months, or actual descriptions of labor and delivery. These writings indicated women's acceptance of pain as punishment, and included the fear and terror they associated with the very real mortality risk for mother and child. These writings also show that in private and profound loneliness, women adhered obediently to conventional impositions of pregnancy and birth; indeed, the very experience was seized from them.

Women were uneasy, anxious, and sick with worry. "Nine months of gestation," says historian Judith Walzer Leavitt, "was always a possible death sentence" (1986, 20). Sylvia Hoffert's careful study of attitudes about birth (1989) reviews personal comments in private writings: Sally Hughes, for example, wrote that she was in a state of "constant depression" (42); Millicent Hunt was "depressed in spirit" (42); and Elizabeth Parker said of her pregnant friend, she "looks so weak and miserable, I dread to see the end thereof" (43).

For many centuries, the phenomenon of birth with its inherent pain represented to both women and men an infliction by God for women's moral frailty. As Cotton Mather threatened in severely solemn and frightening words, childbirth was a serious travail with high mortality risks. According to Mather, mothers might "need no other linnen . . . but a *Winding Sheet,* and have no other chamber but a *grave,* no neighbors but *worms*" (quoted in Hoffert, 64). Slowly recognizing the destruction of the bodies and spirits of women, reformists began the difficult task of changing beliefs about the very nature of women's reproductive lives.

In this chapter we leap forward from centuries of restrictions and obliqueness regarding pregnancy and childbirth to rich, reflexive, frank, and diverse voices that are not silenced as were their foremothers. The selections illustrate the vitality and energy conveyed by Helene Cixous in a parallel she draws between childbearing and writing, urging women to speak of and from themselves so that generative forces of life are released, breaking old patterns and establishing more deeply reflective perspectives:

> She gives birth. With the force of a lioness. Of a plant. Of a cosmogony. Of a woman. She has her source. She draws deeply. She releases. Laughing. And in the wake of the child, a squall of Breath! A longing for text! Confusion! What's come over her? A child! Paper! Intoxications! I'm brimming over! My breasts are overflowing! Milk. Ink. Nursing time. And me? I'm hungry, too. The milky taste of ink! (1991, 31)

BIRTHING BABIES: A WHOLE NEW LANGUAGE HERE

Profound local and systemic changes in maternal physiology are initiated by conception and continue throughout pregnancy.
                        —Laros 1991, 232

During this century a number of events and developments occurred that brought about new challenges and opportunities for women's health. The ability to control reproduction represented new freedoms—and sometimes burdens. Women were no longer in bondage to their households if they chose not to be. Because of public health measures, family size diminished, maternal deaths declined, and newborns thrived. When insurance provided coverage by third-party payers, it became conventional for physicians to confirm pregnancies and enter into routine prenatal care of many women—those covered by insurance, anyway. Except for the poor and the otherwise marginalized who had no choices, North American women embraced medicalized childbirth, and when needed, sought the emerging reproductive technologies for the less than routine pregnancy. Increasing numbers of women were able to manage families and careers; pregnancies were no longer capricious events; parents could be assured of fetal wellness, even gender; and childbirth could be scheduled to meet physicians' preferred schedules. It all sounded so good, until some women began reflecting on the implications of this medical management of their reproductive lives.

As women deliberated on their situations and began to use their own voices to reframe personal experiences, they began to question their loss of power and identity in matters dealing with their own bodies. Jessica Mitford posits in her provocative book *The American Way of Birth* (1992) that in the age of technology, from the obstetrician's point of view

> the ideal venue for a safe delivery was the hospital, where he [sic] would have at hand all the most modern tools and accoutrements, not to mention the convenience to him of having the laboring mothers all in one place where assembly-line efficiency could be practiced. (47)

Still, even though the above scenario is routinely played out in North American hospitals today, an emerging phenomenon in the last half-century has been the movement toward less intrusive medicalized births, evidenced by the following: fewer drugs in labor and delivery; more midwifery and home births; more homelike hospital birth suites; and more family participation (versus more white coats) during labor and birth. These changes are, of course, well-documented in the medical, nursing, and sociological literature, yet fictions, again, are where we find some of the most unabashed, joyful breakthroughs from paternal parameters surrounding childbirth.

As the following stories and poems show, what had been withheld is "uncoiled, released, sprung" (Olsen 1976, 120). These are a kaleidoscope of literary portrayals of pregnancy and childbirth, selected to illustrate how language removed from the universalizing medicalized accounts can return us once again to the local, particular, singular woman telling us about a consciously lived, sensory event in her woman's life, filled with meanings *she* makes.

The number of pregnancies a patient has had is described
with the words gravida, para, and abortus. Gravida 4 (gr4)
means 4 pregnancies, regardless of the outcome. Para 4
(p4) signifies 4 pregnancies carried beyond 20 weeks.
Abortus 3 (ab3) indicates that 3 pregnancies ended before
20 weeks of gestation. A patient with four pregnancies,

three deliveries, and one abortion is listed as gr4, p3, ab1.
                    —Dilts, Green, and Roddick 1979, 67.

Helen Chasin's poem, "The Recovery Room: Lying-In," considers postpartum procedures, an event not generally considered by poets. What used to be discursively off limits or simply deemed inappropriate has become fair game for women eager to describe birth as they have experienced it. Here the speaker's situation is common for hospital deliveries. She has been managed and delivered according to medical protocols; with her "pubic seam stitched back into secrets," she seems "wrapped in scopolamine," unable to "make it out of medicine" (1968, 19). Chasin presents a woman recovering from a medicalized childbirth, an event that now appears hazy, blurred, and disjointed to her. She has been acted upon, supervised mechanistically in an "ordeal that has almost nothing to do with love" (19).

This poetic account is a personal reaction of medicine's imposed production-line model of routinizations, specific timetables, medication schedules, and staff monitorings. The machinelike procedure is uninspiring and numbing, an example of medically managed births: ordeals without love. The poem echoes Regina Morantz-Sanchez's observation that modern woman has been freed by the "industrial order into more sophisticated forms of degradation" (1985, 353).

Carol Nadelson observes that pregnancy has been regarded as the "fulfillment of the deepest and most powerful wish of a woman, an expression of fulfillment and self-realization, a creative act, which affords many women the opportunity to explore new directions in their lives" (1978, 73). While a significant number of women would argue against this extreme elevation of pregnancy in the lives of *all* women, many women would agree that moments of mystery and awe—the first flutter or the outline of a hand in an ultrasound—can momentarily suspend their bodies' weariness.

Sandra McPherson's narrator illustrates some of these moments in the poem "Pregnancy" (1970, 55–56). The narrator describes her condition—not the *news* of her pregnancy, not the *outcome* of her pregnancy, but the *condition* of pregnancy—as "the best thing," so much that she would "always like to be pregnant." And her body: she has a "tummy thickening like a yoghurt,/Unbelievable flower." She is "highly explosive," connected to primordial rhythms, "nine months pulled by nine/Planets." And while she is conscious of and celebrates her sensations of wonder and mystery, she leaves readers with the reminder that she's only one-third of this miracle: "three/Beings' lives gel in my womb."

But in spite of the joy associated with pregnancy—deferred as some of it may be—perhaps no other event in the life cycle is as filled with ambivalence as pregnancy and childbirth. Even for a very wanted or long-awaited baby, the enormous physical changes brought about by pregnancy can temper one's enthusiasm and lead to seemingly perverse ways of thinking. For example, in Joyce Carol Oates's poem "Baby" (1982, 11), the speaker provides an unexpected gothic twist on pregnancy. The title word, seemingly gentle and positive, assumes monstrous proportions as the poem unfolds. Inside the woman, who is merely "four walls and a ceiling," the mollusk-like, sausage-fingered baby grows "filling the room" until no air remains. The baby is all-consuming, carnivorous in its irrepressible growth. The image of the carrier, "a plump wattled purse," is one of entrapment, clearly not a vessel with fragile goods. The poem confounds traditional sentiments about pregnancy and motherhood, brought about by Oates's incisive ability to focus on the unexpected, unspoken impulses and ambiguities that some women might acknowledge during the strange wonders of pregnancy.

Kathleen Rockwell Lawrence's novel *Maud Gone* (1986) portrays a woman's account of pregnancy that also captures the ambivalence of the experience. After years of agonizing, endless conversations of "should we or shouldn't we," Maud settles happily into her first pregnancy at age thirty-three. Clearly the result of a "rational" decision, she nonetheless finds herself late in her pregnancy feeling like a "beached whale," jealously watching her hapless husband watching other women. How had this lapse from the mystical reverie of pregnancy occurred? She and husband Jack, both well-educated, affluent New Yorkers, had done everything right, including their foray into the cult of Painless Birth, Lawrence's cynical label encompassing every method under the rubric of natural childbirth:

> It had been Jack's idea to sign on for Painless Birth. He had read about Xenia in *Business Week:* the remarkable story of her absolutely painless first delivery and how it had inspired her to begin Painless Birth to help other women. Ms. Olssen said there was no pain in childbirth. Pain is in the brain was her refrain, and if that brain were to be filled with images from na-

ture, there wouldn't be any room for pain. It sounded like some Barry Manilow song. (5)

Yet there was another deeper, more intimate reason for Maud's seduction by the litany of Painless Birth: "The promise, false, she knew, but still, a hope . . . the promise of NO PAIN. Maud was a chicken. A real coward. She was terrified of her imminent labor and delivery" (6). She, along with the other "preggers," those of the herniated belly buttons in the middle of swollen stomachs, were trusting, eager, vulnerable to such hope.

Readers find Maud's childish hope laced with cynicism in her inner dialogue as she sits in a Painless Birth class and watches herself, her husband, and the other women and their mates ("one was careful not to say husbands"). The beautiful, svelte Painless Birth instructor asks Maud's husband to pinch and twist ("vary, vary hard. Do not warry bout me. Yust keep twisting" [10]) the back of her smooth, taut thighs to demonstrate how serene one could be in a painless reverie if one just thinks about the ocean. Amazed, angry, and nauseated, Maud rushes to the bathroom. There she sits on the edge of the toilet, resting her head in her arms on the sink, staring at herself in the mirror for a long time wondering where the joy went:

> She stood up and had a good look at her eight-and-a-half-month frame. All stomach, sticking right out there. She had gotten a lot of comments from a lot of folks about that stomach. Pregnancy, Maud found to her chagrin, puts a woman in the public domain. Pregnancy permits no secrets. It's the great common denominator. Everyone knows what it is, and everyone knows how you got that way. People make free with you. Some are solicitous. Some are jocular. Some are outright hostile. And you are pregnant. (13–14)

The class over, Maud and Jack leave, and readers continue to witness difficulties and fantasies and wonder not often found in clinical accounts of pregnancy and delivery. "Think this elevator can handle all you big girls?" (17) one ruddy father-to-be bellows on an elevator after a Painless Birth Class. At that moment Maud hates all men. But while her hatred does not last, her ambivalence does as she wanders through the last days of her pregnancy, still and again the victim of patronizing humor clearly not funny to any woman with a herniated belly button.

BIRTHING BABIES: THE REAL DEAL

*She will begin to hold her breath, tense her ab-
dominal muscles, and strain or bear down in
an attempt to expel the baby each time the
uterus contracts. As this occurs, the relatively
high-pitched cry at the time of contraction
changes to a sustained grunt, which can be rec-
ognized as indicting the second stage whenever
it is heard.*
                                   —Willson 1991a, 377

*A mild cleansing or Fleet's enema may be used
to empty the rectum to prevent fecal soilage of
the delivery area as the fetus descends in the
second stage of labor. While some consider it
"adding insult to injury," the enema gives the
additional benefits of a cleaner field of delivery
and obviation of the need for a bowel movement for a couple of days postpartum. These
advantages seem to outweigh the minor and
brief discomfort early in labor.*
                                        —Fields 1990, 76

In recent decades women visual artists, film makers, and writers have begun a self-conscious exploration of women's bodies, leading to new, different, multilayered understandings of women's
experiences. Formulized pregnancies and deliveries marked by pre-
diction and control have begun to be replaced by more vigorous and
direct images that challenge patriarchic assumptions about wom-
en's reproductive lives. Hélène Cixous's call for *l'écriture feminine*
has been realized in multiple truths by women determined to op-
pose forms of authoritarian discourse, to cross boundaries in literature, art, and film—and in biology and medicine. In spite of ancient
protests of propriety and obscenity that are difficult to unload, pregnancy and childbirth have become rightful subjects of these border
crossings.

In art, for example, Alice Neel's painting of Margaret Evans
has been called the "very incarnation of physical and psychological
vulnerability" (Tobey 1991, 15). Neel's frontally nude and very
gravid woman holds herself erect to convey a sense of pride and tri-

turns, remind us once again that no universalizing explanations exist for these events.

Adoption

In "Unknown Girl in the Maternity Ward" (1960), Anne Sexton's painfully provocative poem, the speaker lingers over her "illegal" child, a "small knuckle" lying on the institutional bed. The mother has carried the child, her "sin," to term in defiance of conventions about unmarried mothers during the period in which it was written. In spite of the hospital's cold and disapproving mood, the beautiful, loving words whispered by this mother to her child reveal the depth of feeling and the ambiguities of her choice:

> You blink in surprise
> and I wonder what you see, my funny kin
> as you trouble my silence. (34–35)

The tender lullaby is interrupted by references to those giving her care in an institution so critical of her situation: wanting only facts, the doctors are "enamel" as staff "scolds" her while she attends to the difficult separation that is her choice:

> I am a shore
> rocking you off. . . .
> Go child, who is my sin and nothing more. (35)

Sexton, an extraordinarily sensitive poet to mood, nuance, and the intuitively unsaid, provides a female narrative voice that struggles with a consequence of pregnancy that is seldom given poetic treatment.

A very different image of an unmarried mother is found in Margaret Drabble's novel *The Millstone* (1965). Here is a woman whose career, we learn in the opening line, "has been marked by confidence and cowardice" (5). As readers come to know Rosamund, they find someone who is well educated, sophisticated, independent, and unmarried. They also find someone who is burdened with a quickly identified millstone: an unplanned pregnancy, which eventually will be transformed from something heavy and oppressive into the "faint, constant and pearly brightness" of baby Octavia (198–99).

Of course, reactions to any particular pregnancy depend on particular circumstances. At first, Rosamund was incredulous and "sat for a whole day in the British Museum . . . thinking about gin" (8) because gin, like quinine and hot baths, might induce an abortion. But her efforts to terminate the pregnancy by such means are foiled: the bath water was stone cold and the gin made her "gay and undespairing" (19). By default, Rosamund chooses to keep her baby without informing the father, who was merely an "incidental" figure anyway. Wavering between poles of confidence and cowardice, she remains compelling *and* unsteady in her lonely course. Once while recalling the tragic plight of Thomas Hardy's unmarried and pregnant Tess, Rosamund confesses:

> Up to this point in my life I had always had the illusion at least of choice, and now for the first time I seemed to become aware of the operation of forces not totally explicable, and not therefore necessarily blinder, smaller, less kind or more ignorant than myself. (77)

Sometimes she is "driven to tears by the sheer embarrassment and absurdity of the situation" (61). Other times she scolds herself that it was nobody's business but her own. Even as cultural patterns enlarge conceptions of "family" to include those with single parents, Drabble's Rosamund reminds us of the difficulties and loneliness that may lace the pleasures of single parenting.

Lisa Woods's poem "Conspiracy" (1980) presents a darker side of adoption from a birth mother's perspective. Much publicity has been given to adoptive children seeking their birth mothers, birth mothers seeking their children. Many have been one-time reunions whereby questions, puzzles, and simple curiosities have been satisfied; others have initiated long-term relationships. But what of the searching birth mother who never finds her child? Woods's narrative voice tells us how one of these women feels:

> Dear child,
> you never happened.
> That's what they'd
> have me believe—
> They drugged me
> during your entry
> into life
> to dull my memory;
> snatched your

newborn flesh
from these unwed arms,
falsifying records
for the sake of Propriety
(and some barren
woman's pride);
denied your existence
to me—
the one
who gave you life—
and turned me out, tainted,
after harvesting
the fruit of my womb
(and called it CHARITY).

And now—
15 years later,
my Soul is bloody
from pounding against
iron Bureaucracies,
trying in vain
to clutch a morsel of proof
that I once had a son . . .
that these
scars on my belly/
wounds in my heart
are not
my imagination.

The narrative voice speaks to her unknown child directly, the child who seemingly "never happened." We quickly learn otherwise, that there is a real baby born and taken from his mother, drugged to lessen the potential connection between them. The authoritative "they," coldly depicted by the mother, seizes the baby from her improper (that is, not married) arms, falsifying records so that someone else could have her child. There is no sentimental connection between birth mother and adoptive mother here; the birth mother uses the loaded word "barren" to describe the adoptive mother whose embarrassment or insecurities over her infertility will be erased when "they" place a baby in her arms. The "they" here—doctors, lawyers, clergy—become her collective and coercive cultural surroundings whispering "shame, shame."

The narrator is bitter at the offenses committed because of her young, vulnerable, naive, and unmarried state, and from their attempts to purge her memory of the experience itself, to cast her out, "tainted / after harvesting / the fruit of [her] womb." But this woman remembers.

Coercion of birth mothers to relinquish their newborn babies is, unfortunately, not a historical phenomenon merely because of today's more relaxed moral codes, the availability of abortion, and the former custom of sending young women away to hide in unwed mothers' homes when dishonor and silence prevailed. Coercive child relinquishment still remains a practice in some areas of the world today (including the United States), and with such practice many birth mothers face lives of pain, depression, and longing.

Thus, it seems, the grief carried around by many women who lived through the physical and emotional trauma of giving birth only to have their babies quickly and quietly taken from them is a grief that is always *there.* In her poem about one woman's abortion, "the mother," Gwendolyn Brooks's narrative voice quietly describes a response similar to that of a birth mother who decides to allow her baby to be adopted: "You remember the children you got that you did not get" (1963, 4).

Infertility

Artificial insemination with donor sperm (AID) requires the wife to realize that a husband's agreement to AID is a profoundly important gift to her.
                                    —Leach 1970, 34

Some women find it hard to attract male partners for whatever reason; others do not lack admirers but fear deep commitment (as symbolised by a genital relationship). Women in either category may understandably wish for a child by donor insemination before it is too late. . . . [yet] I am tired of the argument that no discrimination should be exercised vis-à-vis single women simply because fertile couples can please themselves.
                                    —Humphrey 1991, 798

*It has been estimated that 6,000 to 10,000 chil-
dren are born annually as a result of artificial
insemination and that approximately 10% of
these children are born to single women.*
—*Frank and Brackley 1989, 156*

Matters relating to reproduction are often unpredictable, frus-
trating, and discouraging. A woman's inability to conceive when a
baby is *wanted* can be deeply disheartening, especially if she had assumed that once she made the decision to become pregnant, it
would quickly just happen. Yet often, it does not "just happen," and
women find themselves in painful situations that call into question
their private, sometimes previously unexamined or unspoken, assumptions about themselves and the gendered prescriptions for
their reproductive lives. It is no wonder that when repeated attempts at conception fail, many women turn to medicine to "fix
it . . . *now.*" (Of course, these reproductive technologies are available only to privileged women who have the resources to pay the
high cost of these interventions.)

Susan Sherwin notes that there is a "clear pattern of ever-
increasing medical control over the various aspects of women's reproductive lives" (quoted in Jack, 117–18). By conceptualizing
infertility as a "desperate" state, Sherwin posits that couples "seek
to establish their 'normalcy' and worthiness of treatment by being
eager and compliant thereby verifying the professionals'
stereotypical expectations" (131). Assisted conception, therefore,
strengthens the role of medicine and women's dependence on medical technologies, and raises the persistent issue of male control of
women's reproductive potential.

Over twenty years ago in *The Dialectic of Sex*, Shulamith
Firestone claimed that the perceived female "role" of motherhood
was the very root of women's oppression. This prescriptive function
could be systematically eliminated via existing reproductive technologies that exist and those yet to be developed, such as embryo
gestation outside the womb in an artificial placenta. In this scenario, once the fetus reached full term, any caring person, woman or
man, could attend to its development (Tong 1989, 74), and gendered
roles regarding motherhood would be eliminated.

Similarly, Adrienne Rich made the distinction between the experience of motherhood and the institution of motherhood, the
former being "*women* deciding who, how, when, and where to
mother," the latter being *men* making these decisions for women

Mary Cassatt (American, 1844–1926). *Mother Louise Nursing Her Child*, 1899. Etching with drypoint on paper, 13⅛ × 8⅞ in. The National Museum of Women in the Arts. Gift of Wallace and Wilhelmina Holladay.

(Tong, 87). Men, suggested Rich, have convinced women that unless a woman is a mother, she is somehow not fulfilling her "role." Thus, women often have babies to fulfill prescribed patriarchic gender identity, and when they cannot, they turn to reproductive technologies, another site of ideological battles. Like Firestone, Rich believed institutionalized motherhood should be displaced by women viewing their female biology as a resource rather than a destiny, and not merely *controlling* their bodies, but reveling in the wholeness and resonance of their physicality and the material dimension of their intelligence (Rich 1976, 31–32).

Fictions can enlarge such theorizing by considering various reproductive problems in profoundly personal ways. These fictionalized accounts may bear little resemblance to medical descriptions in textbooks or in the often abstract theorizing about reproductive technologies. Kelly Cherry's "What I Don't Tell People" (1990) is one woman's experience with artificial insemination with donor sperm (AID). Nina, a single, heterosexual woman "of an age that raises the risks [of pregnancy] significantly and who does not earn enough to pay for day care" (202), wants a baby. Without a partner wanting the same, and without a "boyfriend on the horizon," she decides that AID is the best route to go. Reasonably certain that she is able to conceive—she had a miscarriage with a former lover—all she needs is a donor, hopefully with some "good chromosomes," as an enthusiastic friend insisted. The donor is Angus, a friend of this friend, a twenty-one-year-old "whiz kid," handsome, virile, good-natured, generous man who travels quite a distance, taking a week out of his life to help Nina have a baby.

But why does Nina want a baby, now, alone, without much money? She tells the reason directly, with vulnerability, without apology:

> Because I want to hold a baby in my arms, which I have never done in my life. I want to create a life that is independent of mine. I have a hunger for obligations, responsibilities. . . . I always wanted children. . . . I have just learned to drive so that I can chauffeur the kid to slumber parties and swimming lessons. Of course, no one ever asks a married woman to justify why she wants a baby. (202)

So, with Angus's assistance, she undergoes the procedure of AID in her doctor's office.

How does it feel, lying prone, alone with a doctor in an examining room receiving someone's sperm from a syringe? With a nearly detached matter-of-factness, Nina describes the procedure. To the strains of Muzak, the doctor squirts her with a syringe full of Angus's very fresh semen—"fresh" because it can be no longer than a half-hour from his "jack off into the little plastic vial" in Nina's bathroom to her naked-from-the-waist-down state in the doctor's office. After telling her to lift up her bottom so she can hoist her lower body on a platform he extends from the examining table, the doctor leaves the room.

What does she think during those fifteen minutes, waiting alone, motionless? In the absence of lovemaking with a partner during the act of creation, Nina is mindful of her spirit (and possibly that of her future child) during these impersonal, solitary moments of artificial insemination. She has brought two books: one, a collection of poems written by a now-dead friend whose "sweetness of spirit [she] would like for [her child]"; the other, some poems set behind the Iron Curtain, where another man she cares about lives.

Throughout the following days of waiting, Nina leads a rather routinized life: a meeting with a lawyer to sign an agreement full of words like Donor, Recipient, and Parental Rights (Angus has none); a quiet dinner party ("I want my friends to see what good taste I have, to understand that I have not gone bananas and hauled a weirdo in off the streets to impregnate me"); a visit to a bookstore for books on pregnancy and childbirth. All the while she waits and wonders if a baby is "writing its way into existence," her consciousness sensitively turned to the possibilities occurring each moment in her body. It is important to Nina that before Angus leaves he see her "in context." She thinks:

> I want him to understand that I have a nexus, I am part of a community, I may be single but I am not without social meaning . . . my days overlap with the days of my friends like a chain of links. . . . I am not desperate. (209)

Nina is rubbing against the cultural grain here, and her voice helps readers to consider the codes regulating motherhood in North American culture: two parents are inherently better than one; a single woman is selfish (or pathological) if she willfully chooses to have a baby outside marriage or partnership; a single woman raising a child does potential psychological damage to that child. Yet Nina's extraordinary reflectiveness and unhidden vulnerability regarding her decision indicates her membership in that very human tribe of those who want to have and raise a child with no warped agenda and nothing to prove. Drifting to sleep one night shortly after insemination, Nina dreamily thinks: "Although the way I am doing this may not be the right way, or the best way, you can only play the hand you're dealt. This is the only game in town" (212).

More waiting, more weeks. In the bookstore, Nina runs into a woman who has just had her third miscarriage. Nina wonders silently what is wrong with the two of them, two successful women "in a man's world" who cannot seem to accomplish the "most elementary of female roles" (213).

Finally, sadly, Nina begins to bleed. She calls Angus, the doctor, the lawyer, her friends:

> They ask me, now that it seems to be something that is safely in the past, what it feels like to be artificially inseminated. It feels just like what it sounds like, I say: fake fucking. They quiz me for details, which I'm glad to tell them. What I don't tell people, what I never tell them, is that it feels like death. (214)

Cherry's Nina informs readers in this quiet, introspective narrative that a woman's decision to have, or not to have, a baby, is not necessarily tied to relationships with a partner or within a marriage. Whether or not having a baby is "the most elementary of female roles" is certainly open to debate, harkening back to Rich's notion of institutionalized motherhood, "chosen" because of patriarchic ritual, tradition, and custom imposed on women. Yet Nina's *decision* to have a baby (or not) does reflect women's essential right to control their bodies She also helps readers to understand the extraordinarily aseptic nature of this reproductive activity, one that is otherwise so often tied to an act of intimacy and love. While the AID procedure is clinically detached, a woman's body is not. Many questions must be asked by those providing care to women undergoing artificial reproduction: how to be responsive to a woman who feels as though she's "fake fucking"; how to unpack the culturally-induced assumptions about why a single woman, or a lesbian couple, would want a baby; how these factors might influence medical care.

In an unexpected and thoroughly convincing novel that takes place in the too-near future, Margaret Atwood's *The Handmaid's Tale* (1986) is a frightening, tyrannical turn to the problem of infertility. Set in an ultrapatriarchy that fuses God and government, the novel takes readers to the Republic of Gilead where, among other social ills, the declining birthrate has humiliating, dehumanizing, and terrifying consequences for many women. In this society, a handmaid is a (hopefully) fertile woman, a vessel whose singular purpose is to have babies, but not just any baby: the fathers must be Commanders, members of the militaristic, patriarchic government. If and when Commanders' wives are or become infertile, the handmaids do it for them, attempting conception each month in a macabre ritual called the Ceremony.

The narrative voice, Offred (literally, "of Fred"), describes the Ceremony in a language that far exceeds any businesslike, clinically detached surrogacy scenario one might have envisioned. In the Commander's bed, his wife is arranged, outspread, legs apart. The handmaid, here Offred, lies between the wife's legs, her head on the wife's stomach, face up, the wife's "pubic bone under the base of [the handmaid's] skull" (93). Both women and the Commander are fully clothed. The handmaid and the wife hold hands, signifying they are "one flesh." But what it means, the handmaid observes, is that the wife is "in control, of the process and thus the product" (94). Offred describes the procedure:

> My red skirt is hitched up to my waist, though no higher. Below it the Commander is fucking. What he is fucking is the lower part of my body. I do not say making love, because this is not what he's doing. Copulating too would be inaccurate, because it would imply two people and one is involved. Nor does rape cover it: nothing is going on here that I haven't signed up for. There wasn't a lot of choice but there was some, and this is what I chose. (94)

What makes Atwood's tale so coldly, cynically despairing is its close approximation to the United States's contemporary political/ religious phenomenon of the New Right and its vision for women and notion of family. The continued threat to reproductive rights along with advances in reproductive technologies make the story almost plausible. The detachment of mind from body in both the believable Cherry account and Atwood's futurist vision reveal a potential cost to the soul for moving conception into the laboratory or into the legal arena of surrogacy. When health care providers and policy makers, when *women* examine the benefits of reproductive technologies, important questions remain. Where is a woman's spirit in all this? How is it being tended, and by whom? What is the effect of separating body and feeling? Who benefits from these technologies, and whose interests are being served? Offred's cold observation of her purpose is worth recording here as we reflect on these questions:

> We are for breeding purposes: we aren't concubines, geisha girls, courtesans. On the contrary: everything possible has been done to remove us from that category. There is supposed to be nothing entertaining about us, no room is to be permitted for the flowering of secret lusts. . . . We are two-legged wombs, that's all: sacred vessels, ambulatory chalices. (136)

Abortion

The decision to abort should be made early,
preferably before the end of the first trimester,
so that the pregnancy can be interrupted safely
and in the simplest way—by suction curettage
or, when necessary, formal D & C. A variation
involving vacuum aspiration of the uterine con-
tents (an office procedure) within 14 days of a
missed menstrual period is also widely prac-
ticed and has been termed menstrual regula-
tion or menstrual extraction. . . . Only 3 to 4
percent of women so managed during early
pregnancy require further treatment because of
method failure.
    —Clarke-Pearson and Dawood 1990, 345

Judith Wilt (1992) perceptively writes that "debate about abortion may begin with reasons and proceed to statistics, but it always comes down, really, to stories" (20). And many of these stories reflect the aftermath of the abortion, "even when the narrative supports the structure of choice" (20). Why is this? Wilt maintains this refusal of the narrator to stop thinking about the conception comes "only partly from the novelist's moral universe; it comes most deeply from the demands of narrative itself which irresistibly imagines endings for characters' lives beyond the story's last pages" (21).

This abortion aftermath is evident in the following fictionalized accounts of abortion, selected not to imply that all women
think incessantly about that event. Rather, these were selected to
embody one dimension of abortion that may be experienced by
some women, and to provide a way of thinking about postabortion
deliberation without confusing it with guilt.

Some abortion fictions get right to the point by announcing
the subject directly in the title. Alice Walker's short story, "The
Abortion" (1981), concerns the relationship of Imani and Clarence,
contemporary, upscale African-Americans living in a small south-
ern town in the United States. Clarence is a legal advisor to the new
African-American mayor, and is dedicated to his boss's success. It
appears that life is good for Imani: she and her husband are re-
spected (even though the mayor ignores her at social functions);
their two-year-old child Clarice is flourishing; her husband has always seemed the "best human being" she had ever met.

The first sentence in the story enunciates the problem set
forth in the title: "They had discussed it, but not deeply, whether
they wanted the baby she was now carrying" (64). This is the thread
that begins to unravel the story beneath the seemingly smooth surface of her life, marred just now with an unplanned pregnancy. She
is ambivalent about another child and Clarence is more interested
in his position with the mayor than with the nuances of their marriage, which she found boring within its first year. There had been a
painful miscarriage after Clarice's birth, and earlier when in college
she had had an abortion (pre-Clarence) that she thought of as "wonderful, bearing as it had all the marks of a supreme coming of age
and a seizing of the direction of her own life" (67).

Clarence does not try to persuade Imani to keep the baby she is
carrying, nor does he counsel her to have an abortion. She alone decides to have an abortion, which she must travel to New York to
have. With alarming insensitivity, Clarence invites the mayor with
him when he drives Imani to the airport, deep in conversation with
him all the way about "municipal funds, racist cops, and the facilities for teaching at the chaotic, newly integrated schools" (66–67).
In spite of her emotional fragility at the time, Imani is secondary to
the political chatter; she could have easily been going to the dentist.
Not surprisingly, she drifts back to her first abortion, the kindly
Italian doctor who performed it, and his parting comment, "And
when you leave, be sure to walk as if nothing is wrong" (68). She
also remembers hemorrhaging steadily for six weeks, and that she
was not well again for a year.

But that was then, and now is seven years later. Abortions had changed, having "entered the age of the assembly line." At the abortion clinic, ready for the procedure, Imani is

> grateful for the lack of distinction between herself and the other women—all colors, ages, states of misery or nervousness—she was less happy to notice, once the doctor started to insert the catheter, that the anesthesia she had been given was insufficient. But assembly lines don't stop because the product on them has a complaint. Her doctor whistled, and assured her she was all right, and carried the procedure through to the horrific end. Imani fainted some seconds before that. (69)

She is taken to a peaceful room full of cheerful primary colors. A kindly, white-haired nurse takes care of her and tries to reassure her about the way she looked ("gray as if all her blood had leaked out") and that she would be "fine in a week or so" (69–70). But then, still with the immediacy of what had just occurred, Imani could not imagine being fine: "Somewhere her child—she never dodged into the language of 'fetuses' and 'amorphous growths'—was being flushed down a sewer. Gone all her or his chances to see the sunlight, savor a fig" (70). But Imani had made a decision, and it was her own: "Well," she said to this unborn child, "it was you or me, Kiddo, and I chose me" (70). Sometime later when she decides to leave Clarence, she understands the very moment, "the exact second," when the marriage had taken an irreversible turn, even if "no perceptible mark" had been left. The moment was the abortion, reflecting her isolation and loneliness, and Clarence's lack of empathy for the enormity of her feelings.

Walker's story widens the lens of understanding on this incendiary issue. Imani's situation and actions reflect no patterns of behavior associated with the current religious/political debate. This woman is privileged, responsible, well educated, and married, a profile that frustrates commonly held notions of who gets abortions (no matter that most legally induced abortions tend to be performed on women who [1] are young, white, and unmarried, [2] have no previous live births, and [3] are having the procedure for the first time [Koonin et al. 1990, 23]).

Another perspective on abortion is Lucille Clifton's "the lost baby poem" (1987b, 60), a bittersweet and courageous poem written in the narrative voice of a mother to a child she had aborted in the past. At first, the words "lost baby" in the title imply a miscarriage, as in "she lost the baby." But when readers move down to the first line of the poem, the narrator tells us that she "dropped" her unborn child's "almost body" down into the toilet, the words "i dropped" suggesting a more purposeful act. Even if the act was a carefully thought-out decision, the narrator has not forgotten the event years later ("what did i know about waters rushing back"). Now, years later, she wants to tell the conditions of her life then that prompted her decision, *not* as an apology to her unborn child, but as an explanation.

The second stanza begins, "you would have been born into winter / in the year of the disconnected gas / and no car," a clear sketch of her inability to care for a baby financially. But the words that follow leave little doubt of what her intentions were had the baby been born: "we would have made the thin / walk over genesee hill into the canada wind / to watch you slip like ice into strangers' hands," that is, adoption.

The final stanza is a dedication, perhaps a rededication of the mother/narrator to being a parent deeply committed to her children. In memory of the never-realized child to whom she is talking, she pledges:

> if i am ever less than a mountain
> for your definite brothers and sisters
> let the rivers pour over my head
>
> . . .
>
> for your never named sake

Within the economy of a poem, Clifton's narrator illustrates that it is possible for women to grieve the loss without regretting the decision, a critical distinction and understanding especially in a culture waiting to seize such personal decisions from women.

As the preceding stories indicate, for *some* women abortion is not a simple matter, nor is it over when it is over. In *The Women of Brewster Place* (1982), an extraordinary novel about seven women living as neighbors in a tenement on a dead-end street, Gloria Naylor portrays the seeming dead-endedness of their lives. The book includes seven stories of women who endure incredible pain of merely living, and the likewise marginalized men with whom they live— uneducated, jobless, and demoralized—who, in turn, victimize them. The book is also a collective story of survival and deep affection between women, as survival comes to mean relying on each other. Set in an environment of daily despair, the narrators unflinchingly portray a human society struggling against repressive forces of racism, poverty, dependence, and unspeakable loss. With remarkable resilience and spirit, these women connect with each other to maintain small fragments of hope.

Lucielia Louise Turner's story focuses on an abortion, but like many stories on that subject, it is not about a smooth, straight-up decision; rather, it twists to become a tangled and complicated event. Her husband, out of work and defeated, provides none of the love she needs; instead, his relationship to her is characterized by selfishness and abuse. Lucielia's joy in life comes from Serena, their daughter who toddles along "on plump uncertain legs"—the only thing she "ever loved without pain." Eugene, the mean-spirited husband, fiercely resents Lucielia's friendship with Mattie, an older neighbor who comforts her with "huge ebony arms" and who Eugene sees as an interfering "fat bitch."

When Eugene chooses to come home, he expects to be waited on and served obediently. When he wants sex, she willingly consents to the "raw urges that cre[ep], uninvited, between her thighs on countless nights; the eternal whys all meshed with the explainable hate and unexplainable love" (91). In spite of such visits, he is an unreliable spouse: "the last eleven months of her life h[a]ng compressed in the air between the click of the lock and his 'Yo, baby' " (91). Now she is pregnant, wanting this child, knowing that the news will bring angry reproaches and will force a decision she does not want to make. His reaction is predictable: "Another brat comin' here, huh?" and later, "I'm fucking' sick of never getting ahead. Babies and bills, tha's all you good for" (94). Ciel has no chance, no life of her own. Like other desperate women, she is driven to choose between her husband or partner and her child.

When the physician tells her, "Nothing to it, Mrs. Turner," we know better. A practiced monologue of the matter-of-fact procedure:

> Please, relax. I'm going to give you a local anesthetic and then perform a simple D and C, or what you'd call a scraping to clean out the uterus. Then you'll rest here for about an hour and be on your way. There won't even be much bleeding. (95)

As the physician "droned on" with "sterile kindness" Ciel paid no attention. By imagining another woman controlling her actions, she keeps herself isolated from what was happening to her and to the fetus she was losing:

> Ciel was not listening. . . . All the activities of the past week of her life were balled up and jammed on the right side of her brain, as if belonging to some other woman. And when she had endured this one last thing for her, she would push it up there, too, and then one day give it all to her—Ciel wanted no part of it. (95)

After the abortion Ciel feels disconnected; Eugene, always insensitive, continues to badger her, calling her a "moody bitch." Suddenly, she cannot bear to be separated from Serena, and seldom lets her from her sight.

Naylor's story could end at this point. But the tragedy of Ciel's life is compounded at the moment "when the poison of reality beg[ins] to spread through her body like gangrene," when she sees Eugene for what he really is, "a tall, skinny black man with arrogance and selfishness" (100). Just as she decides to escape with Serena, who is "someone who love[s] her," the child wanders into another room busily following a roach as it races across the room to find "security in the electric wall socket under the kitchen table" (98). The curious child picks up a fork and pushes it into the deadly outlet.

Ciel's grief after the funeral is not only for Serena; "she [is] simply tired of hurting" (101). Mattie, watching Ciel give up, dying before her eyes, responds with love, the only resource she has to offer:

> She rocked her into her childhood and let her see murdered dreams. And she rocked her back, back into the womb, to the nadir of her hurt, and they found it—a slight silver splinter, embedded just below the surface of the skin. And Mattie rocked and pulled—and the splinter gave way, but its roots were deep, gigantic, ragged, and tore up flesh with bits of fat and muscle tissue clinging to them. They left a huge hole, which was already starting to pus over, but Mattie was satisfied. It would heal. (103–4)

Naylor's narrative portrays the unique ways that poverty, need, and scarcity can bear down on poor women caught in economic dependencies. Wilt observes that "having the power to choose when to engage maternity, and how much maternity to engage, is paradoxically essential for keeping black *women* alive" (25). Such was Ciel's "choice," far too tangled in the particularities of her sad and noble life to be reduced to the chants of current political/religious debates, charted here in the ambiguities and agonies of the women of Brewster Place.

A final narrative voice is that of Maria, the narrator of Joan Didion's *Play It As It Lays* (1970), who undergoes what was at that time an illegal abortion in the United States. Surprisingly, the doctor's litany is the same as those in the cheerful, efficient legal clinics fictionalized by Walker and Naylor: "This is just induced menstruation. . . . Nothing to have any emotional difficulties about, better not to think about it at all, quite often the pain is worse when we think about it. . . . relax, Maria, I said *relax*" (82).

Maria's postabortion life wanders on, marked by the malaise and disorientation Didion often develops in her characters. Her life is as it has always been, anesthetized against sorrow and joy, touched only by her neurologically damaged daughter, and finally by the realization of her abortion.

Months after the event, after an annoying encounter with an agent, she gets into her car and drives until she must pull over. She rests her head against the steering wheel and cries "as she had not cried since she was a child" (141). She cries for her mother, her daughter, her humiliation with the agent, and finally, she realizes something else she is crying for:

> She had deliberately not counted the months but she must have been counting them unawares, must have been keeping a relentless count somewhere, because this was the day, the day the baby would have been born. (141)

Such is the abortion aftermath Wilt describes; the narrative cannot leave it as one more event in the narrator's sleepwalking life. For some women it is a significant event, and it must be acknowledge as such. This is not to suggest that acknowledgment necessarily implies pain or regret. In fact, Alice Walker declares that the college friend who found her a doctor to perform a prelegal abortion "handed [her] back [her] life." During that week, she "wrote without stopping almost all the poems in *Once*" (Wilt, 20). What these fictions tell us is that an abortion, that choice itself, is not necessarily a sterile decision or a singular moment in time, but may be a collection of moments weaving in and around the event, over time and space, patterned by a full range of human emotions.

TARPAPER ROOMS

Women of color and women who are poor have often been more profoundly affected by the medicalization of childbirth. In fact, such women are often invisible. Deprived of social, political, and economic power, these women frequently face subtle and overt abuse in hospital and clinical settings reflecting the added layer of racism and classism enacted by the already sexist medical culture. Yet many women of color have shaped into fictions their particular trials and celebrations of pregnancy and childbirth.

"Eyes," a poem by Lucille Clifton (1991c, 21–23), is not about the physicality of birth, but about inequities and deprivation. Here she speaks of an African-American girl giving birth "somewhere in Alabama" in a "tarpaper room." Obstetrics/gynecology texts do not refer to such birthing rooms, but Clifton's description forces disturbing confrontations with the circumstances of birth for marginalized women. The deprived, shivering girl sings a song of guarded hope amid no timetables, no white-jacketed supervision, no medication. Clifton lays out fragments of a story that reflect a disturbing reality: if white women have been managed and controlled, women of color have often been ignored. As several North American women of color dramatically illustrate in the following narratives, "only through knowing one another . . . can we know ourselves" (Martin 1990, 7).

However variously marginalized, women understand the difference between respectful and abusive care. The portrayal of Pauline, a laboring African-American woman in Toni Morrison's *The Bluest Eye* (1970, 98–99), is one such example of brutal, dehumanizing "caregiving." Pauline, ready to give birth to her second child, decides to go to the hospital rather than have it at home as she did with her first so she could be "easeful." While the story takes place over fifty years ago, readers may be startled by the cruel overtness of the racist doctor who, at Pauline's bedside, remarks casually to the doctors rounding with him, "These here women you don't have any trouble with. They deliver right away and with no pain. Just like horses." She is teaching material, a faceless body for learning about medicine: the "old one was learning the young ones about babies," she informs readers. Without looking her in the eyes or addressing her by name, the physician demonstrates professional abuse as he jellies his glove and rams his hand between her legs. Because Morrison endows the patient with eloquent words for describing how she is treated and how she feels, readers are stunned by the doctor's lack of respect and compassion and his glaring professional arrogance.

Only one of the younger doctors looks at Pauline in the face, and when he does, she knows that he is ashamed at what he has just witnessed. He knows, Pauline thinks, that she is no mare foaling, but he moves on with the rest of them as they begin examining a white woman nearby, fussing over her, asking her how she was doing. Pauline's pains get worse, and she starts moaning "something awful" even though the pains are not as bad as she is letting on. But she needs to let everyone know:

> I hurt just like them white women. Just 'cause I wasn't hooping and hollering before didn't mean I wasn't feeling pain. What'd they think? That just 'cause I knowed how to have a baby with no fuss that my behind wasn't pulling and aching like theirs?

Of course, such flagrant racism at the bedside might be harder to find today. But Morrison's Pauline and the doctors caring for her may confront caregivers to examine their unspoken beliefs about illness and pain filtered through race, ethnicity, and class, and how these beliefs are enacted in their treatment of patients.

An engaging contrast to Pauline's hospital experience is found in Mary Helen Ponce's "La Doctora Barr" (1987). This story is a chronicle of how birth occurred in a small California barrio, written in a first-person narrative by a woman recounting the mysteries and rituals of childbirth she witnessed as a child. Dr. Barr (also "Señora Barr" or "Mrs. Doctor"), a physician from the nearby city of Burbank who cared for most of the women who lived in the barrio, was usually not consulted by pregnant women until well into the final month, because "most of the women had an idea of what to do during *un embarazo*. . . . [They] continued with their work, caring for home and children until the first labor pains" (113). Once the pains began, a neighbor rushed off to a pay phone to summon Dr. Barr while the other neighborhood women brought out the clean sheets, put water on to boil, and scattered the children so that when Dr.

Barr arrived everything was ready. The laboring woman would be lying in a bed of clean white sheets, have her face washed and her hair pulled back, and have in her hand a clean rag to bite on when the pain became too much. Here, screaming out was considered to be *muy ranchera,* a disparaging term for less sophisticated, "country" people; the women in this barrio did not want to appear this way, thus the clean rag.

The story is brimming with rich traditions formerly practiced in this small barrio. *La dieta,* for example, practiced by women after giving birth, pertained not just to food, but to customs practiced by new mothers: not bathing for six weeks after the birth in order not to catch a cold; wearing a heavy *banda,* strips of old sheets wound around her stomach immediately after childbirth to ensure that *la matriz* would contract and return to its normal size. Moreover, no heavy housework was permitted: "this was a time when a woman like my mother who worked hard most of her life was allowed to rest and be waited on by family and neighbors" (115). But like many rites and rituals, *la dieta* was modified or abolished as the lives of women in the barrio changed. In time they too were up soon after birth doing their work and caring for their families.

This story does not take place in a tarpaper room. Yet the story illuminates how childbirth was enacted in sites outside hospitals, outside the loop of traditional medicalized births where, in a community of women caring for other women, childbirth was an unadorned yet deeply significant event filled with tenderness, and in an absence of technological accoutrements.

Toi Derricotte's series of poems in *Natural Birth* is an unwed girls' account of the last part of her pregnancy through her delivery. The narrative voice finds herself, because of the too-full maternity house in "another city," with the Reynolds family. The girl ceaselessly watches and wonders about this quiet family who has opened their home to her, wondering in particular about the young wife/mother, "what she thinks, feels, who she is" (14). In spite of the family's unquestioning acceptance of her, she still feels alone, a stranger.

At the beginning of her ninth month, she travels to a maternity ward for unwed girls and women. There she decided to have Lamaze—"i didn't need a husband or a trained doctor—i'd do it myself" (19). When her water broke, she was reminded that it was she who always told the others to "be tough, to stop believing in their mother's pain. . . . it wouldn't hurt like we'd been told. birth was beautiful if we believed that it was beautiful and right and good!" (21).

But once in the labor and delivery quarters, "everything conspired to make [her] feel afraid" (22). Her pain is foreign, relentless, insufferable. Her caregivers offer no solace. The doctor on duty is a caricature of the unfeeling physician:

> doctor come in, wrenches his hand, a hammer up my cunt. wants to feel the head, wants to feel the damn thing's head, wants to see how far i am. . . . FORGET ALL THAT SILLY BREATHING STUFF. YOU'LL TAKE A SHOT LIKE THE REST WHEN THE TIME COMES. now, every time he sticks that wooden board up me, jams that stake inside my bleeding heart, i know, this is one who likes to give me pain. (25)

She thinks the doctor is "happy" to make her feel such pain, happy because he is a man and in control of her. Using the language of rape, the girl tries but cannot "move away from him while he takes [her] on this bed of pain," telling her it is for "her own good," that it is "almost over" (27). She believes he wants her to beg for release from pain, but she does not, keeping her "pain locked up inside. he'll never know how much he hurts" (27).

Finally, in the delivery room, out of control with pain, exhausted, the same abhorrent doctor demands to give her a spinal. At last she submits:

> i put my belly in my hand
> gave him that
> thin side
> of my back
> the bones
> intruding on the air
> in little knobs
> in joints
> he might
> crack
> down my spine
> his knuckles
> rap
> each twisted
> symmetry

put me on
the rack,
each
nerve
bright
and stretched
like canvas. (40)

But before it is too late, "dr. y," the head obstetrician, breezes in, asks her if she even wants the shot, is told no, and says "PUT YOUR LEGS UP, GIRL, AND / PUSH!" (41). Such is the beginning of her mystical, shining, end-stage labor. Left to her own instincts, she proceeds to "grow deep," a phrase she uses repeatedly as she moves in and out of her body, now suspended above her body, watching, startled that she is so beautiful and full of light. But the spell is broken: someone starts demanding, relentlessly: "NAME PLEASE / PLEASE / NAME" (45). The baby is born—"the sudden visibility / his body"—but she does not know him: "who / is this / child?" He is now the stranger, in spite of the note he brings with him with the word "mother" inscribed.

Now, back in her room, she is "neither virgin nor mother." She prepares to leave the hospital and begin her task of coming to know her son, a "thing she had to discover," and herself, in the "body of a stranger" (53). But what of those other girls in the ward?:

where did those girls go after the births of their babies? What wind blew them away like ashes? those she loved well, without question; those she was taught not to believe in . . . where did they go when they were flat and empty, when they fit back into their old clothes? (55)

Wherever they went, they went silently after "dressing hurriedly in the dark" after the papers were signed. And the narrator's final flashback to the birth experience for these young women: "most had asked to be blindfolded" (55).

The fictions in this chapter portray the multilayered dimensions and issues surrounding pregnancy and childbirth. From early oblique references to tentative, courageous descriptions, to the raw, unprocessed immediacies of lived experiences, these narratives widen medicalized frames of such experiences. Wilt (1992) summarizes what literary renderings of pregnancy can do:

> Pregnancy, of course, is the ultimate surprise, the roof lifting just as you've finally got the doors and windows closed. Artists can make this malleable surprise play in dozens of ways. The narrative or the character within the narrative can define pregnancy as the proof of true womanhood or manhood, the reward or punishment of God, the fruit of good or bad sexuality, the sign of a relationship knitting or sundering, the extension, transformation, exposure of the self which projects the pregnancy. The definition will radically color the climax of the pregnancy narrative, whether it is birth or termination, and whether that narrative is a case history or a work of art. (21)

Suzanne Valadon (French, 1865–1938). *Girl on a Small Wall*, 1930, 36¼×29 in. The National Museum of Women in the Arts. Gift of Wallace and Wilhelmina Holladay.

Chapter 2

Coming of Age

*Female pubertal changes start between ages 8
and 13 years and changes take place for 3 to 4
years. Breast development commonly precedes
pubic hair development. Most girls reach adult
height midway through puberty. . . . More than
half (60%) of teenagers surveyed while receiving routine health care indicated that they experience depression as frequently as once a
month to daily. Women experience depression
more commonly than men. . . . poor self-image,
including dissatisfaction with one's physical
appearance, lack of self-confidence, and a hope-
less vision of the future, may contribute significantly to depression.*
                    —Dworkin 1987, 76, 87–88

The years between girlhood and adulthood are characterized
by enormous physical and emotional changes that bring strange and
mysterious transformation to a girl's body. Maturing biologically
into womanhood is, in contemporary United States culture, often
suffused with ambiguities: the season is a rite of celebration and joy,
and a passage full of vulnerability, apprehension, and confusion.
The changes associated with physical maturation—onset of menstruation, development of breasts, growth of pubic hair, widening of
hips, and increasing awareness of one's sexuality—all represent

more than biological transformations. These changes have everything to do with a young woman's identity, her values and beliefs
confronting and commingling with those of the prevailing culture,
her present desires and future vision of herself-as-woman.

Because they provide visual documentation, mirrors assume
new importance. So do friends, families, and strangers on the street
as observers whose eyes and expressions inform a young woman
about her changing body. Looking back on this time as a period of
confusion and wonder, many adult women feel happy just for having
survived more or less intact the challenges and difficulties of adolescence in a sexist, consumerist culture. Many women remember
that very first show of blood, wearing their first bra, becoming aware
of their bodies' new and foreign scents, plus experiencing all the
anxieties associated with dating, touching and being touched, their
own and others' sexuality, all laced with a general sense of awk-
wardness, self-consciousness, and self-distortion. Many would not
recall or characterize this as an easy period.

When women gather, personal stories often unfold to reveal
memories of this passage that range from humorous to tragic. Such
narratives reflect confusion and shyness; others tell of violence,
abuse, and enduring pain; others record days or moments of over-
whelming emotional discomfort. Frequently these coming-of-age
reflections are viewed from the vantage of mothers studying their
daughters. In Sharon Olds's *vanitas* poem "35/10" (1983, 75), a
mother brushing her daughter's "dark silken hair" is jolted by the
sight of her own grey hair in the mirror, which causes her to muse
about the child's becoming and her own ending:

> Why is it
> just as we begin to go
> they begin to arrive, the fold in my neck
> clarifying as the fine bones of her
> hips sharpen?

This is, the mother notes, "the story of replacement." Just as her
own skin begins to dry and her body "snaps its [reproductive] clasp,"
the daughter's "purse" fills with "eggs, round and firm as hard-
boiled yolks." The mirror brings the "oldest story" into focus, a moment when loss and renewal are captured simultaneously.

In this chapter we look at fictions that deal with young wom-
en's physical/sexual development and some of the events associated

with this period of change. Some of the biological events are shared by all women; others are violent acts imposed on unwilling victims, part of the ongoing, global brutalization of women and girls; others are historicized phenomena that reflect many young women's obsession with body image, most notably thinness. Collectively, the narratives reveal sensitivity, vulnerability, humor, affirmation, pain, and confusion. They reveal not the physiology of adolescence, but rather what comes with those bodily transformations—the myriad desires and apprehensions of becoming a woman.

DISCOVERY

Dysmenorrhea ("difficult monthly flow") . . . is experienced by the majority of adolescents. Prevalence among the adolescent population approaches 60%, and it is the leading cause of school absenteeism among young women.
                              —Wilson 1990, 722

Popular language used to describe menstruation tends to cast it as a negative event women must endure: "on the rag," "the curse," and so on. More current is the pejorative use of PMS, a trendy, sophisticated label that translates into predictable degradation. Children sitting in front of television sets are bombarded with advertisements relating to female "troubles," the need for medication, tampons, and douches, thereby linking this odious dimension of femaleness with inconvenience, shame, and sickness.

Such beliefs start early in a girl's life, not merely in ubiquitous media incantations, but sometimes in the beliefs, spoken and not, passed from mothers to daughters. Even when communication is relatively open and good between mothers and daughters, girls sometimes have difficulties receiving practical information for reducing anxieties about insertion of a tampon, use of a pad, odor, spotting and staining. Although sex education programs are available in schools, "girls are herded into the auditorium and shown a film, generally produced by one of the sanitary napkin and tampon manufacturers, in which butterflies flitter through uteri and in which menstruation and the need to use these various products are explained" (Madaras 1991, 60).

Toni Cade Bambara is one of several writers who have created an honest, explicit, fictionalized account of this entrance to biolog-

ical maturity. Bambara creates Rae Ann, a young African-American
girl, at the precise moment when blood mysteriously and inexpli-
cably begins to flow from her body. In the appropriately named narrative, "A Girl's Story" (1977), this unprepared adolescent is in a
state of terror, confused and frightened by the red stain in her panties. Adults know this to be a natural event in female biology, but for
a totally uninformed girl, the bright spot is shocking. Rae Ann
counts to twenty, hoping to stop the blood by magical conjuring and
incantations. It does not work. She thinks hard about other possible
remedies. Remembering that with nosebleeds "you put your head
way back and stuff tissue up your nostrils" (152), she "hoists her
hips higher toward the wall" (153). It does not work. She tries other
solutions: "ice cubes on the neck, on the stomach, on the thighs.
Had stuffed herself with tissue. Had put her hips atop a pile of sofa
cushions" (153). Nothing works, and the bleeding continues. She
panics about the trail of drippings between the toilet and bed, worrying about the towels she has ruined and the "panties and skirt
she'd bundled up in the bottom of the garbage" (153). An accompa-
nying odor further increases her misery:

> Rae Ann was smelling herself and not liking it. She'd already
> counted three sets of twenties, which meant is was time to
> move. She rejected the notion of a bath. The last bath had only
> made it worse. Fore she could even get one foot good out the
> water, red spots were sliding off the side of the tub onto the tile.
> (156)

Clearly, Rae Ann had not been prepared, and needed immediate help
and reassurance. She thought of Dada Bibi, the "shiny-faced
woman" over at the Center:

> [She would] know exactly what to do . . . would talk calmly.
> Would help her. Would tell her there was nothing to worry
> about, that she was a good girl and was not being punished.
> Would give an explanation and make things right. But between
> the house and the Center she could bleed to death. (153)

In the meantime, before leaving the privacy of her bedroom and
bathroom for the Center where Dada Bibi could help, she needed to
sort things out, to get organized:

[She] exhaled deeply and tried to make a list in her head. New tissue, tight pants to hold it all in place, the last of the ice tray still in the sink on her twat. She closed her eyes and moaned. Her list was all out of order. She tried again. Check floors and tub. Put towels in bottom of garbage. Put garbage out. Scrape carrots and make salad. Secrete a roll of tissue in her closet for later. (156)

Rae Ann's dilemma, her confusion, her fears may prompt women readers to remember their own first moments of this experience: the uncertain joy, perhaps embarrassment, a hesitancy in telling someone or seeking help. Or Bambara's story may provide graphic details and confrontations that are *outside* readers' experiences, that cannot be similarly told in medicalized or psychologized terms. Rae Ann's innocence during the first moments of her period is given to us in earthy, evocative language, summoning memory and identification for some female readers, and perhaps an enlarged understanding for male readers:

Rae Ann pulled her legs down and swung off the bed. She checked to see that the newspaper was still in place before drawing the covers up. She stood and parted the flaps of her bathrobe. Last time she moved too quickly oozing had started, a blob of syrupy brown slipping down the inside of her leg and she afraid to touch it, to stop it, just stood there like a simpleton till it reached her ankle, and then she fled into the bathroom too late. She was looking into the toilet as the water swirled away the first wad of tissue. What if the toilet stuffed up, backed on the next flush. She could imagine M'Dear bellowing the roof down as the river of red overran the rim and spilled over onto the tiles, flooding the bathroom, splashing past the threshold and onto the hall linoleum. (157)

Language like this is what girls do *not* often get when learning about menstruation from their mothers, older women, the school sexuality curriculum, their doctors. They are usually told about the shedding of the uterine wall, or about the menstrual cycle, often with admonitions of varying degrees regarding their new reproductive capacities, with more fear, more shame. Yet the raw details, the ones Rae Ann does not censor, are the ones girls and those who care for them would benefit from hearing—suspending anatomical/

psychological talk long enough to *feel* with a girl what it is like to stuff herself with tissue, watch in fear or shame a blob of syrupy brown slipping down her leg, or see the trail of her own drippings on the floor. Still, even in contemporary United States culture where sexuality is infused in everything from breakfast cereals to bathing to beer drinking, discussions of menstruation often occur with lowered voices in euphemistic language, while pads and tampons remain where they have always been—under the cabinet, in the purse, out of sight.

Bambara's account is rich with tenderness, misery, and humor: the brother banging at the bathroom door ("We know what you been doing"); M'Dear (her grandmother) screaming, "What you been doing?" And then, "Don't tell me nothin when I'm trying to find out somethin. Miz Gladys run all the way up to the bus stop to tell me she seen you comin home from the school way before three o'clock." And Rae Ann feeling trapped: "If she unhooked the roll of toilet paper to take into her room," it would be noticed, and besides, "the smell was in everything. In her bed, her clothes, her breath." She screamed, "Don't come in here," and began to cry (157–59).

When the frightened girl finally comes out of the bathroom, she does not know what to say to soften the accusations in her grandmother's voice. The reader is tenderly, empathically connected to Rae Ann's innocent, scared, simple truth, "I'm bleeding." M'Dear's response is numbing, not the sympathetic, bittersweet reaction of an older woman whose child/grandchild has just experienced what could be a connective, gendered rite of passage. Looking "red-hot and strangled," as if ready to slap her cornered granddaughter, she hisses:

> Whatcha been doing? . . . You been to the barbershop haven't you? Let that filthy man go up inside you with a clothes hanger. You going to be your mama all over again. Why didn't you come to me? Who's the boy? Tell me his name quick. And you better not lie.

This exchange explains, perhaps, why the girl has not been prepared by her grandmother: keep her ignorant, then no harm can come to her. We can assume that Rae Ann's mother had become pregnant, had a botched abortion, and died, leaving M'Dear to care for the two surviving children. Bits and pieces of the story start to fit together as subconsciously, in an insensitive, suspicious environment, deceased mother and daughter come together. Rae Ann's strong repulsion to the smell of blood, her own normal discharge, reminds her of death:

> The smell of her mother's sickroom years ago, so long ago all the memory that had survived was the smell and the off-yellow color from the lamp, a color she'd never ever seen again anywhere.

M'Dear finally, slowly grasps the truth, exclaiming, "Girl, why didn't you say so?"

Rae Ann's predicament, especially her lack of information, does not seem to reflect today's savvy teenagers who have myriad sources of information, so much of it highly sexualized in film, television, advertising, magazines, and books. Yet many may still find themselves in similar states of confusion and distress, possessors of a vocabulary—ovum, uterus, lining, egg—but having no idea of other girls' lived experience of this important passage: the sight of the bright red stain, the spot on the back of a skirt, the dull abdominal ache, the odors, the unexplainable shame at being discovered. After all, even in highly sexualized cultures, young women have been schooled to cover and protect their genitalia—and often with good reason, given the systematic violence against women sustained over time and across cultures.

Bambara's story reveals more than the onset of menses. Here three generations come together at a critical moment to provide a historic review of some of women's reproductive difficulties: the grandmother's failure to inform; the mother's desperate and fatal abortion; the daughter's continuing belief patterns of female biology as something secretive yet powerful, natural yet mysterious, exalted yet slightly shameful.

Other narratives offer different experiences of this event. Ellen Bass's poem, "First Menstruation" (1975, 50), presents a narrator who has "been waiting / for what felt like a lifetime" for her period to start. Unlike Rae Ann, she *knows* what is supposed to happen and waits impatiently for this important moment; once she even pretended that her period had started. When at last the sign did appear in her panties, she "carried them to [her] mother, hoping, unsure, afraid—Mom, is this it?" The narrator *appears* well informed and close to her mother, who demonstrates an efficient, matter-of-fact response when she provides pad and belt, even showing her how to wear them, casually inviting her to "come to

me, ask me," when she has questions. After all, "you can ask a
mother anything."

Just then the girl realizes that she is alone, even in the presence of her mother and her mother's friend Dot, and the bond that
might have existed between her and her mother is quite ethereal:

> The three of us
> standing in the bedroom
> me, the woman-child, standing with the older women
> and the feeling
> there once was a feeling
> that should be here,
> there once was a rite, a communion.

At this significant moment marking physical maturity, she realizes
that the communion she had expected is limited to proper use of pad
and belt. Other elixirs were not included in this exchange, and are
not likely to occur in the future: "I said, yes, I'll ask my mother /
but we all, except maybe Dot, / knew it wasn't true." The long-
awaited physical event is shadowed by the daughter's realization
that an intangible gap exists between her and her mother, a separation that is not bridged by this new biological connection. The
mother's provision of sanitary products answers the physical demands, but does not touch the unarticulated emotional needs of
this young woman. She wants more, just as Rae Ann desperately
needed more.

Both young women are in similar straits: they need someone
to tell them/talk to, yet in both instances, the support figures fail.
But we cannot totally fault these caregivers for the nature of or lack
of their nurturing; mothers/mother figures are constantly receiving
conflicting messages from their adolescent daughters surrounding
mother-daughter intimacies, issues of independence/dependence, in
the midst of a burgeoning sexuality. Apter (1990) puts it this way:
the developing young woman "wants the mother to watch and ap-
preciate, but not misunderstand, to watch and see and understand,
but not to intrude, to allow individuality, to be enthusiastic and
confident about growth and maturity, yet not to let go, not to forget,
and above all not to abandon" (121).

A different perspective on the onset of menstruation is found
in Cynthia M. Zelman's short story, "Our Menstruation" (1991).

The subtitle, "for the girls," is further enunciated in the first sentence, "we menstruated simultaneously," suggesting that the story can be read as a historicized account of girls becoming women, and not just merely those in the story.

The narrative voice is that of a woman looking back, telling the story from her memories, pulling readers back to those sixth-grade norms many of us from that time and culture may have forgotten: deference to boys, shame/pride in our changing bodies, intimacy and envy between and among friends, fears of being different, and many more. The story begins with the narrator and her friends showing off for uninterested boys, keenly aware of the physical changes that she and her friends are experiencing:

> We'd started out as very young children but we would leave as near adolescents, woman-sprouts. And then on to junior high school, that bastion of filth and first pimples, pubic hair and plunges from innocence. (461)

The narrator is watchful, an insider chronicling the nuances of change:

> We had our first period, *together.* Okay, the actual blood flowed from only one of us upon the great event of our first menstruation, but we shared the experience, most of us unwillingly, some of us traumatically. Collective menstruation it was: like a ritual, like a virgin thrown to the gods. We gave something up to get something back: blood for womanhood. We did not quite understand the event, yet we sensed a monumental purpose. Our menstruation was big. (461)

The story, with its title, first line, and first paragraph (preceding reference), with the repetition of plural pronouns, leaves little doubt about its subject. And, as readers discover, the story of "our" menstruation, *was* big.

It is the story of Vicky, a metaphorical figure, who was both an outsider and a larger-than-life figure. Disdainful, proud, and confident, Vicky was "full of purpose and strength," oblivious to flirting machinations that have permitted inflated kickball scores by boys, the "silent compact, an agreement to play less well than we were able to make the boys love us." Vicky interrupted these demure affectations by playing skillfully and decisively, slamming balls in for victory. While the other girls deferred to the boys, establishing early patterns of domination and diminishment, Vicky swaggered, unashamed of her size and power.

The critical event, the onset of Vicky's period, occurred during a baseball game when all eyes were focused on her Amazonian powers. The clutch of boy-obsessed girls cringed with embarrassment over her ungainly appearance and determination to excel. For them, she was an invader, an unwelcome, unappreciated explosion of unfemininity. At the decisive moment of the game when the bases were loaded, Vicky took her place at bat, ready to score more than just the winning run. As the spectator-reader learns, the grand slam she was about to deliver is twofold:

> Vicky was wearing red-and-white checkered stretch pants. Those pants are unforgettable. God knows what size they were but to our self-conscious eyes they were huge, a red-and-white checked tent, an awning over a barbershop, something to sell hot-dogs and beer under at the fair. Finally, Michael rolled the ball toward her and as Vicky lifted her left leg for real, we saw it: a large patch from her midthigh to her crotch where there were no white checks: just a large sea of red, a red deeper than the color of her pants, a red deeper than a Crayola crayon. Red like a Delicious Apple. Red like a sundae cherry. Red like the Devil. Red as Hell. (465)

The girls, distracted from the ball sailing high over the fence, watched with mortified horror the public display of Vicky's first period. Lynne Stark reacted quickly, running toward second base, trying to intercept the triumphant batter, screaming, "Vicky, you got to go to the nurse." Vicky responded characteristically:

> [She] hesitated a moment, looked at us, looked down between her legs and yelled back "Nah," and damn it if she wasn't going to run all around those bases with our first blood dripping down her thighs. (466)

The boys responded variously: they did not understand, they giggled, or they turned away; the girls were "as red in the face as Vicky was in the thigh." Within minutes, however, the girls understood that Vicky had made "her last home run, or her first as a woman." As she leaves the field, Vicky shakes her "right fist two or three times in the air." For the remainder of the day, all sixth-grade girls keep "checking [their] pants or skirt to see if it was staining blood."

Vicky, big as an earthquake, comes to symbolize womanhood for these girls, moving them to some slightly higher plateau of understandings about being women, being together. She remains constant to herself and her unspoken beliefs about gender, never submitting to the small deceits and deference of her peers.

DISSATISFACTION

Nothing is more common among adolescent girls, and indeed developing women of all ages, than to accentuate physical dissatisfaction, to feel they would be much better off if only certain things about their appearance were different.
                                     —Apter 1990, 24

Bulimia is episodic binge eating, often accompanied by purging, and is rampant among adolescent and young adult women.
                          —Strasburger and Brown 1991, 474

The ideal: pretty, of course. Nice skin. Stylish clothes and hair. But the absolute requirement for the female body during adolescence (and beyond) is this: to be thin at all costs. Fat is ugly. Fat is repulsive to others. Fat makes one unlovable.

These beliefs begin formation at quite a young age. Indeed, often very young children believe weight control to be synonymous with self-control and attractiveness:

> Children as young as six years rate pictures of endomorphs negatively, and pudgy children are frequently subjected to ridicule and exclusion. . . . Female appearance is so important . . . that when pictures of women are manipulated to increase their bust size, they are viewed as being less intelligent and competent than women with smaller busts. It is not surprising . . . that some researchers believe most women are at risk for developing some degree of eating disorder. (Strasburger and Brown 1991, 475–76)

"Skanks," a short story by Rennie Sparks (1990), illustrates how terrifying and painful adolescence can be when lived according to the relentless standards of physical attractiveness. Many readers can identify with the teenage narrator Janine, who is overweight and unattractive: either we knew her or we were her. Adding to Janine's inability to live up to these standards is a fractured and disjointed family, which makes Janine even more fragile and tragic. While she copes with her insensitive stepfather, her best friend Dawn faces a self-absorbed mother (called Lorraine instead of Mom) who focuses only on herself and the "optometrist she met at work." Dawn and Lorraine form a cruel but all too familiar teen pairing, one attractive, the other ungainly and disposable, a friend until something better comes along.

From the onset Dawn is all-knowing and self-assured; Janine is not and badly wants to be accepted and included:

> Dawn and me eat scrambled eggs with tomato juice because we're on a diet. Dawn knows how to make herself throw up so she eats toast and butter too. I eat only English muffins because my fingers go so far down my throat, but nothing comes up. I'm a fat cow. (61)

The bulimic ritual of gorging and forced vomiting is in preparation for Dawn's current mission in life: "going to the Mall to fall in love." Janine, whose stepfather has declared her "a pig for eating all his cocktail onions," needs a nurturing relationship *somewhere* in her life, but her friendship with Dawn is hardly the kind of supportive connection that helps her deal with her negative self concept. For her, mall cruising is not a happy prospect.

As a tag-along best friend, Janine gets ready with Dawn for the Mall. Preparation includes lying "down flat on the bed next to each other to zip [their] jeans," swallowing several of Lorraine's Dexitrims, and fluffing their hair. Finally, they wrap sanitary pads in tin foil to put in their purses, Janine observing that "since I've been sleeping over, we get our periods at the same time. With tin foil around the pads we can open our purses in public and not have some skank scream, 'Look, she's on the rag' " (62).

At the Mall Janine's cultural narrative continues to reveal superficially, banality, and desperation as the girls dash into the bathroom for still more fixing up:

> Dawn doesn't like the way her hair turned out so she wets it in the sink and kneels under the hand dryer, one knee on the tile

floor, to do it over. I look at myself in the mirror. My hair and nails are perfect. I know how to copy the looks, but my cheeks are full and red, not hollow and sharp like Dawn's. Tomorrow I will eat nothing but cocktail onions. (62)

Janine wants to be like the others, but in spite of her own self-loathing and the clear disregard from her more attractive peers, she is honest, sensitive, and more interesting. Yet affirmation is nowhere to be found, especially with Dawn's hurtful abuse ("Janine, look at yourself in a mirror sometime. You think you can do better than Stevie?") regarding a humiliating sexual experience with a sleazy boy named Stevie who, minutes after their first meeting, pushes her face into the zipper of his jeans saying, "Hey, come on, baby. . . . What are you on the rag or something?" (64).

The story ends with Janine by herself, back at the Mall. She becomes aware of her aloneness, then immediately seeks comfort at Anthony's, where she buys three pieces of pepperoni pizza. In spite of her unsuccessful bulimic attempts, she runs to the restroom at Sears to try again, turning on the hand dryer so no one will hear her:

> I lean down over the bowl, one hand holding on to the toilet paper roll. The other hand turns into a knife and I stick it down into my throat until my stomach starts to shake and my mouth gags open wide and the pizza rushes back up my throat. . . . I lean against the wall of the stall, my head against the coat hook. My stomach feels thin and flat, empty. And just for one second I feel beautiful. (64)

Such is the allure of thinness to an overweight adolescent who believes—because everyone/thing tells her so—that with thinness comes acceptance, popularity, love. The sad, pathetic act of bulimia is not too great a price to pay for these promises.

VIOLENCE: THE DARK AT THE TOP OF THE STAIRS

It is important for the physician to understand
the various patterns of sexual abuse in order to
provide good medical care. The feelings aroused
by such cases can be uncomfortable for the
physician; reactions range from anger to fasci-

*nation with the course of events. The clinician
needs to . . . remain calm and nonjudgmental.*
      —Emans and Goldstein 1990, 543

Women have always been at risk for sexual violence by predators ranging from close family members to total strangers. Sexual
abuse of minors is a crime abhorred and vilified by most societies,
past and present, but has been and continues to be tolerated, ignored, minimized, and even covered up in practice. The heinous-
ness of sexual molestation, incest, and rape is defined by Susan
Brownmiller in her brilliant work, *Against Our Will* (1975):

> To talk about rape, even with nervous laughter, is to acknowl-
> edge a woman's special victim status. We hear the whispers
> when we are children: *girls get raped.* Not boys. The message
> becomes clear. Rape has something to do with our sex. Rape is
> something awful that happens to females: it is the dark at the
> top of the stairs, the undefinable abyss that is just around the
> corner and unless we watch our step it might become our des-
> tiny. (343)

For young girls, rape is inculcated into female notions of danger very
early in life. "Little Red Riding Hood," for example, is a "parable of
rape" (344), suggesting along with other fairy tales and myths that
terrible harm befalls little girls unless they are saved by a hunter, or
(if they are lucky) a prince.

In the following examination of two poems and two novels,
we present perspectives that do not dismiss the victim of rape or
perpetuate distorted blaming-the-victim proverbs. These fictions
suggest that sexual violence is more than a minor and transient haz-
ard for young women; whether a child is victimized once or repeatedly, the psychological damage is traumatic and often tragically
enduring.

Increased reporting of child abuse shows that the emphasis on
outside or nonfamily perpetrators inaccurately targets the smaller
group of offenders. In fact, *intrafamily* assaults pose greater and
more common dangers to young children and adolescents. In Orr's
study of one hundred sexually abused children who were between
the ages of one and fifteen, the victim knew the offender in 74 percent of the cases, and in 50 percent the offender was a relative (cited
in Emans and Goldstein, 539). Those are the statistics; what do fictions tell us about these crimes to the body and spirit?

Jane Smiley's novel *A Thousand Acres* (1991), *King Lear* with a shocking twist, portrays the enduring violence of incest to the body and spirit. Ginny Cook (Goneril), the narrative voice, tells the story of her family, a wealthy farmer and his three daughters. The similarities to Lear are obvious: the old man is impetuous and foolish; two daughters, Ginny and Rose, seem rather self-absorbed; Caroline, the youngest, exhibits Cordelia-like candor in her reactions and relationships. When the novel opens, the world is secure: the thousand acres are well-managed, seemingly prosperous, even idyllic for the widowed father and his two older daughters who live just across the street in their own homes. Or so it seems.

As the story unfolds, Ginny's childlessness (which includes five miscarriages) and Rose's cancer become tragic emblems for the world they occupy. That is, the soil on the largest farm in Zebulon County appears fertile and productive, but in fact is contaminated and unable to sustain life. Ginny submerges her pain by efficiently tending to her husband's needs, baking, gardening, and caring for her father, a bullying old man who lives alone. In spite of Ginny's dutiful attention, which includes daily preparation of meals and general housekeeping, the widower is surprisingly distant, difficult, and unappreciative. But to Ginny his behavior is normal.

Unlike her sister, who suffers complacently, Rose seethes with inexplicable anger. Although she is recovering from a mastectomy, the rage she expresses seems to derive from other wounds. Of the three daughters, only Caroline has moved on to another state where she practices law. Ironically, the independent, detached daughter, who seldom visits and supplies no domestic comforts to the father, is his favorite.

Smiley's story explores family relationships and the hidden roots that shape and define behaviors and conflicts, some lasting a lifetime. The disclosure of a horribly dark secret explains, perhaps, the personalities of the three daughters, and in the case of Ginny and Rose, their metaphoric afflictions. The matter-of-fact references to Ginny's infertility and Rose's breast cancer, both sex-specific, provide the first clues about the perversions that took place in their motherless childhood home. While Ginny and Rose mothered and protected their younger sister and assumed domestic responsibilities, they also substituted for their mother in another terrible way. Rose forces Ginny, who has blocked the evil from her mind, to recall the oppression imposed upon them by their father that now accounts for one sister's strange passivity and the other's unceasing rage:

"Ginny, you don't remember how he came after us, do you?"

"Came after us?"

"When we were teenagers. How he came into our rooms."

I licked my lips and switched my legs so the right crossed over the left. I said, "We slept together while Mommy was sick."

"And then, that Christmas, we moved into separate rooms. He said it was time we had separate rooms."

"Well, of course, I remember having separate rooms, I don't remember why."

"He went into your room at night."

"What for? I don't remember that at all." (188)

An incredulous Rose demands, "How can you not remember? You were fifteen years old! . . . He was having sex with you" (188–89).

Ginny's denial conforms to the secrecy and suppression described by Burgess and Holmstron (1978) whereby the traumatic incident or "unresolved issue," so long "encapsulated within the psychic structure," will, upon disclosure, produce strong emotional effects. Shortly after the confrontation with Rose, Ginny goes to the linen closet and to her childhood bedroom to find her past, discovering that the folded yellow sheets trigger recollections she had tried to erase:

> The sheets fit smoothly over the single bed in the yellow bedroom. . . . I folded back the top edge over the blanket. . . . The dressing table was beside the window; the closet door was ajar; the yellow paint on the empty chest was peeling; some bronze circles floated in the mirror; a water spot had formed on the ceiling. Lying here, I knew that he had been in there with me, and that my father had lain with me on that bed, that I had looked at the top of his head, at his balding spot in the brown grizzled hair, while feeling him suck my breasts. That was the only memory I could endure before I jumped out of the bed with a cry. (228)

Ginny's shocking epiphany flows out of her subconscious, the memory of her father's violent betrayal blighting the land and its owners.

Smiley's novel is layered with rich complexities, but none more powerful and astonishing than the core event, the sexual vic-

timization of two vulnerable teenager girls who, as their story unfolds, are permanently scarred. Through such a reinterpretation of
Lear, Smiley demonstrates the cost of this hideous form of the domination of women and girls.

In her brilliant analysis, *The Creation of Patriarchy* (1986),
Gerda Lerner reminds us that none of this is new, that "biological
and cultural factors predisposed men to enslave women before they
had learned how to enslave men. Physical terror and coercion . . .
took, for women, the form of rape" (87). And through the ages, rape
has remained "nothing more or less than a conscious process of in-
timidation by which *all men* keep *all women* in a state of fear"
(Brownmiller, 4).

Rape occurs every 10 minutes in the United
States, yet a majority of rapes are unreported.
                    —Griffith-Kenney 1986, 237

The patient with acute trauma will
demonstrate perineal contusions or lacerations
and hymenal tears with bleeding, fissures,
erythema, and discharge. . . . Emotional trauma
varies with the age of the victim and the cir-
cumstances of the assault.
                    —Barkin and Rosen 1990, 162

While Smiley's lengthy novel provides thick, lengthy descriptions of characters and events, Sharon Olds's three-stanza poem entitled "The Girl" (1987, 14–15) is a graphic, highly-imaged portrayal
of rape achieved in a relatively small number of words, leaving readers with a searing, lasting impression of a rape incident involving
two girls. Two twelve-year-old girls are chased through the woods
by a pair of men, who finally catch them in a small clearing. The
"thin one with black hair" starts raping "her best friend," while the

> blond one stood above her,
> thrust his thumbs back inside her jaws, she was twelve,
> stuck his penis in her mouth and throat
>   faster and faster and faster.

Not yet satisfied with their savage assault, the two predators stand
up, staring at the naked bodies of the girls, one of them savagely tell-

ing them, *"Now you're going to know what it's like / to be shot 5 times and slaughtered like a pig."* The men switch places, and continue the barbaric violation. As the violence peaks, the blond one stabs her friend as he rapes her, while the black-haired one is with the other girl, "sticking inside her / in one place and then another." She feels the point of his gun in her waist, then "a little click in her spine and a / sting like 7-Up in her head." Everything, then, goes dark.

In stanza two, the surviving child who has been left for dead regains consciousness, sees the body of her dead friend, and begins to run. "Like a wound debriding," she flees from the woods, crossing the field over to the railroad tracks, and says pitifully to the railway brakeman, "Please, sir. Please, sir."

Stanza three presents the aftermath: the trial; her new, heinous, unwanted knowledge; and the need to go on, to survive. When asked in the courtroom to describe what happened to her, "she had to say everything," using words her big sister taught her, sitting in the same room with the two men, pointing them out when she was asked.

Yet life continues for her. Numbly, she goes to parties, does her math, does not smoke, cheerleads, does dishes, prays for the soul of her dead friend, and thanks God for life. Throughout it all, she is possessor of "what all of us never want to know." Olds, of course, has told us what we don't want to know either, about the dangers in the woods and what exactly the wolf can do.

The final selection does not deal with direct physical violence leveled against girls. It does, however, illustrate the emotional impact of sexual abuse in the form of exhibitionism, whereby a child may be aware of sexual meanings yet naive and unskilled in their implications. Even though such incidents may not involve overt physical contact, the emotional effects of this abuse can be extremely injurious.

Julia Alvarez's novel, *How the Garcia Girls Lost Their Accents* (1991), concerns four sisters embarked on two concurrent journeys: one from adolescence to adulthood; the other from a comfortable, predictable life in the Dominican Republic to an uneasy resettlement in the United States. In addition to the normal difficulties associated with growing up, political turmoil abruptly uprooted the lively young women from their native land with its Hispanic culture and extended family life, forcing them to struggle with a

strange language and even stranger culture. Circulating stories told
by each sister, Alvarez's collection cuts back and forth in time and
place, shifting from childhood experiences on the vibrant Caribbean
island to pubescent years and beyond in the Bronx and elsewhere.

On the first anniversary of the Garcia family's arrival in the
United States, the family celebrated with a cake and a request for
wishes. Carla, now in her early teens, closed her eyes wishing,
"Dear God, let us please go back home, please" (150). The occasion
allowed Carla to contrast the pleasures of her remembered island
home with the hardships she faced at school and in the neighborhood. It also stirred her to recall events, one in particular, that produced misery and fear.

At school Carla suffered jibes about her foreignness by
boys who also enjoyed badgering her about her body's changing
appearance:

> Every day on the playground . . . a gang of boys chased after her,
> calling her names. . . . "Go back to where you came from, you
> dirty spic!" One of them, standing behind her in line, pulled
> her blouse out of her skirt where it was tucked in and lifted it
> high. "No titties," he snickered. (153)

Mortified and hurt, she begged them to stop in her newly acquired
yet faulty language, speaking words and phrases that further incite
their harangues. Carla hated to go to school to face children who
were

> disclosing her secret shame: her body was changing. The girl
> she had been back home in Spanish was being shed. In her
> place—almost as if the boys' ugly words and taunts had the
> power of spells—was a hairy, breast-budding grownup no one
> would ever love. (153)

As if this kind of abuse from cruel peers were not difficult enough,
Carla's distress increased, this time by an exhibitionist.

One day on her way home from school, Carla realized that she
was being followed by a car driven by a "grown-up American man
about her parents' age" who beckoned her to walk over to his car.
Insecure about her ability to use proper English, Carla was appre-
hensive, fearing she would be unable to provide the directions he

must surely want. Yet she noticed "something wrong" with the man's smile, which had a "bruised, sorry quality as if the man were someone who'd been picked on all his life, and so his smiles were appeasing, not friendly" (156). Then, something caught her eye:

> She looked down and stared, aghast. . . . The man had tied his two shirtends just about his waist and was naked from there on down. String encircled his waist, the loose ends knotted in front and then looped around his penis. As Carla watched, his big blunt-headed thing grew so that it filled and strained at the lasso it was caught in. (157)

Carla's mouth drops and she backs away while observing that the intruder's face now shows a "pained, urgent expression" as his arm "pumped at something." Finally his "face relaxed into something like peacefulness," and Carla runs home (157).

At this time Carla seemed to have only a dim sense of what has happened. The police are called and a terrifying interview begins. The interrogators are impatient with her reticence and her inability to provide answers in English. They want specifics: What kind of vehicle? What did he look like? What was he wearing? What did you see? Carla cannot give accurate descriptions, and is embarrassed by many of the questions. When one of the officers demanded gruffly, "A string?", Carla saw that the policeman's face was

> an adult version of the sickly white faces of the boys in the playground. This is what they would look like once they grew up. There was no meanness in this face, no kindness either. No recognition of the difficulty she was having in trying to describe what she had seen with her tiny English vocabulary. (163)

For Carla the boys in the playground blur with the deviant in the car and the policemen into a fearful amorphous shadow. In order to sleep at night she closes her eyes and wishes them gone, replaced by those with whom she felt loved and safe:

> In that dark she created by keeping her eyes shut, she would pray, beginning with the names of her own sisters, for all those she wanted God to especially care for, here and back home.

The seemingly endless list of familiar names would coax her back to sleep with a feeling of safety, of a world still peopled by those who loved her. (164–65)

In such preadolescent experiences, it may be that the interrogation is as disturbing as the actual incident; in Alvarez's fiction, for example, more text is given to the trauma of answering questions than to the actual event. The subtext of this interrogation has more to do with the questioners' doubts, indifference, or insensitivity to the event rather than overt contempt for the victim—we hope.

The patterns form early, these cookie-cutter-perfect, Barbie-doll standards for girls, certainly coded well before adolescence but inscribed more relentlessly there, and with a higher price for deviance from these physical norms. And if these standards are not difficult enough for girls to work toward, the physical changes and ambiguities so charged with sexual awakenings, insecurities, and confusion make this coming-of-age a complicated, difficult physical and emotional labor.

Add to these patterns the ubiquitous, never-ending threat of violence to all who are born female, and what we find are girls and women engaged in lifelong searches for ways to live without fear and shame—in bodies that are theirs, in a world full of choices, in the company of those who see them whole.

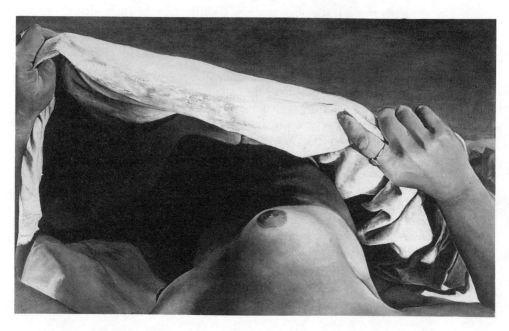

Joan Semmel (American, b. 1932). *Woman Under Sheet*, 1974. Oil on canvas, 48×78 in. The National Museum of Women in the Arts. Gift of Gertrude B. Drake.

Chapter 3

Breast Cancer

Breast cancer is a medical and a life crisis.
  —Snyderman and Snyderman 1987, 531

Margaret Mead's study of various cultures led
her to conclude that breasts are so idealized in
the United States that they are the primary
source of female identity.
  —National Institutes of Health 1979, 56

Particular types of cancer can arouse distinct
psychosocial concerns in the patient. For exam-
ple, fear of loss of femininity and mutilation
were found in Quint's study of mastectomies.
  —Enelow and Devine 1982, 270

Perhaps no other disease summons the kind of dread in women than that evoked by even the mention of breast cancer. Currently in North American culture, breasts are a symbol of femininity and sexuality. Attention via dress or undress is given to breasts everywhere: in films, videos, and magazines; in offices, schools, markets, and malls; on posters and billboards. Breasts are visible under plunging necklines, wet T-shirts, tight sweaters, tiny tank or halter tops, and bikinis. These archetypal breasts, covered or uncovered to some extent, are smooth and firm. The message is relentless: breasts are very feminine, very sexy. And the pursuit/maintenance of firm breasts is a constant in the lives of many contemporary women. We lift weights, buy bras designed to lift or enlarge, and (for the very privileged) even go to the dramatic and often dangerous extent of undergoing breast augmentation.

It is no wonder, then, that a woman diagnosed with breast cancer is terrified. She is terrified because of the sharp double edge of facing a potentially fatal disease, and of losing a precious part of her body that is deeply tangled in her sexuality, femininity, self. Often she is furious, and her fury, along with that of other women similarly stricken, is diffuse and multilayered:

> Should we . . . lash out at the political and social problems around us that might have created a place in our breasts where stray, mutant cells implanted themselves and began their deadly progression? . . . What about the doctors who examined us year after year, felt . . . lumps and assured us that they were "nothing"? Or should we attack the surgeons whose knives actually severed our breasts from our bodies? . . . [Perhaps] the anger is aimed at the breast cancer as a disease whose treatment requires tearing a woman's breast from her body. (Kushner 1988, xiii, xv)

These are deep and significant feelings that cannot be medicalized into neat stage theories, changed by treatment plans, or normalized by upbeat assurances that "of course you don't equate your femininity with your breasts." Breast cancer and mastectomy are experiences that evoke angst, and most women who live through it "have a desperate need to share their feelings with others" (Kushner, xiv).

Breast amputation is mutilating; it alters a woman's body. Particularly significant is the fact that it affects a part of her body intimately associated with sexual fulfillment and child-bearing. Concern with appearance after surgery may be mitigated only partly by the use of prosthetic devices. The change in her body is one that the woman herself must learn to accept and cope with, regardless of what measures she may use to conceal the disfigurement from others.

—Scherer 1991, 703

"Amputation . . . mutilation . . . disfigurement": with words like these found in the medical/nursing literature, what must health providers think the experience of mastectomy is like for women? With women's breasts part of the cultural codes of femininity and sexuality, of course psychologic trauma of some kind is a predictable response for women who have undergone mastectomy. But women learn to cope in highly individualized and idiosyncratic ways, dependent, for example, on the nature and sources of their self-esteem; their values and beliefs; their partners, friends, and families; the nature of sexual intimacy in their lives. Thus, the imaginative literature we have selected reflects a wide range of response of women who have faced breast cancer and mastectomy. Yet the often highly abstracted clinical language gives little insight into a woman's lived experience of breast cancer.

Thus, our move to imaginative literature may reflect a far wider range of response of women who have faced breast cancer and mastectomy. There is, of course, initial fear and sometimes denial that anything is wrong. Once the mastectomy has occurred, women sometimes experience shame and often sadness with their changed bodies. Yet some women somehow transcend the experience, a transcendence that can occur during the shock and fear of diagnosis and treatment, or later after they have lived awhile in their different bodies. Leatrice Lifshitz proposes that

> the challenge of breast cancer and mastectomy is the challenge of change—not the slowly evolving change that we associate with life, but the cataclysmic change that drops like a death sentence and forces us into being who we are not. (1988, xvii)

The stories and poems that follow do not presume to portray the final word or some universal experience of breast cancer as do, perhaps, many clinical descriptions. But they may enlarge our understanding of how some women live through their experience of fear, anger, loss, and recognition.

THE BEGINNING: DENIAL AND FEAR

Several studies report that women find the
time between finding the lump and diagnosis
the most psychologically stressful part of the
whole experience.
—Fallowfield and Baum 1991, 1083

Women who refuse to participate in breast self-
examination tend to be:
(1) Afraid that cancer will actually be found
(2) Fearful that such a finding will destroy her
*   life*
(3) Feel that they should not go looking for
*   more problems than they already have.*
                    —Jakobsen, Beckmann, Beckmann,
                              and Brunner 1987, 75

An early study . . . identified two groups of pa-
tients with symptoms who had delayed con-
sulting a doctor: ignorant of the implications of
their symptoms. . . [or] overwhelmed by fear of
doctors, hospitals, illness in general and cancer
in particular that they delayed reporting their
symptoms.
                    —Fallowfield and Baum 1991, 1083

The lump is found. Who finds it? A woman, alone in bed, or in
the shower, or dressing in front of a mirror. With her heart racing,
her fingers disbelieving, what does she think? No, she may tell herself over and over again, it must be something else. She makes an
appointment with her doctor, or perhaps she waits, hoping whatever
she felt disappears tomorrow, next week, next month.

But fear does not necessarily begin with a palpable mass or the
appearance of an irregularity in a mammogram. The nagging fear
may begin earlier when a woman no longer feels immune: when a
mother, sister, grandmother, or friend gets breast cancer; or when
her doctor urges a baseline mammogram. Linda Pastan's (1985)
poem, "Routine Mammogram," depicts the vulnerability a woman
may feel during this procedure, one that feels anything but routine:

> We are looking for a worm
> in the apple—
> that fruit which ever since Eden
>
> has been susceptible
> to frost
> or appetite. (46)

The perfect, ripe, sensuous apple is violated by an ugly, loathsome
worm that invades the beautiful fruit. Her vulnerability is what she

is thinking about during this routinized procedure—the fact that her precious breast-fruit has become a site of possible invasion. With an easy formality the friendly doctor shows the patient the pictures that she sees as "aerial photographs, / moonscapes / of craters and lakes" (46). But the patient sees more—the "faults" that she "might fall through one day" or "valleys where every shadow / could mean total / eclipse" (46). This woman is half-listening; she's doing her own imaging of potential flaws in the landscape of her breasts, and of

> ... Amazon women
> with just one
> breast,
>
> their bowstrings
> tightening
> for war. (46)

The mammogram turns out predictably normal: "You're fine," the doctor tells her, smiling. But the patient knows that she is changed. She has seen the fragile faults deep in her body, and she knows that no one, not her doctor, not even with his reassuring diagnosis, can "give innocence back,"

> as if he could give back
> to the apple
> its spiraled skin. (47)

In Safiya Henderson-Holmes's "Snapshots of Grace" (1990), we find a denial so deep that it may cost a woman her life. Arranged by discrete sections labeled "photographs" ("fifth picture: color, group shot" or "thirteenth picture: black and white, overexposed"), the story is a chronology of Grace from age five to her present middle age. The snapshots give readers selected access to Grace's life, here at five looking in "her mama's bedroom mirror . . . her blouse is above her chest, two perfectly round, perfectly mahogany-brown circles stare at her" (331–32). Several years later we find her asking, "Mama, am I gonna have real big titties like you and Mrs. Warren?" (332). More years pass, then one day while looking in the bedroom mirror, turning left, then right: "Mama? Mama? Ooooh Mama, I really, really need a bra" (335). As she grows into womanhood, Grace

receives many messages about her large breasts, about the importance of women's breasts, from girlfriends worrying about crooked
or asymmetrical breasts ("How would we get a husband then?"), to
her mother admiring "the way that bra carries" Grace, to her husband, Ben:

> "I sure love snugglin' right here in the middle of 'em."
> "You sure do."
> "Like to feel 'em on my cheeks and nose, so soft and warm."
> "I like it best when you touch 'em with your fingertips real
>   slow, like. . . ."
> "Like this?"
> "Yeah, especially the left one."

How does one remain immune from such affirmation? Certainly
Grace does not.

Well into middle age with almost-grown children and busy career, Grace visits a doctor who finds something suspicious and orders an immediate biopsy. Grace does not follow up, and a year
passes before she returns to the clinic where a young doctor, seeing
that the biopsy had not been performed, asks her if she had it done
elsewhere. "Ah, no, I didn't," Grace answers. The doctor remarks,
"A year, huh. Any pain, discomfort?" "A dull kind of pain, just
sometimes." "Discharge?" the doctor asks. "It's probably nerves,"
Grace replies, "but last month I noticed a slight something coming
from the left one. I don't know" (334).

During the same visit, more questions. "Why didn't you come
back in and see about yourself?" Grace: "It was a busy year, work,
my mother was very ill" (335). Then, hours later during the same
visit, bad news. "Mrs. Williams, you've got a rather large mass in
your left breast." Grace closes her eyes and says, "That's what they
told me last year. I guess—I guess all year I was hoping it would dis-
appear or move down to my big toe or something." But the doctor
has more: "Grace, you have a smaller one in your right breast, too."
Grace: "So what did it have, a baby?" (337).

The story ends after her surgery with Grace talking to her
daughter Aisha sitting at her bedside, Grace fretting that she missed
Aisha's graduation. Grace turns the conversation to Aisha's graduation dress, worrying if she wore a bra: "Your father is going to send
some of those pictures to his folks, and you know how they are"
(342). And the cycle goes around again: breasts are brashly cele-

brated, or quietly hidden treasures. Yet, for Grace her breasts were more than sexual appendages that warranted admiration from others, visual affirmation of her womanness, or sexual enticements. They were her body, her self; removal of her breast was not simply removal of a peripheral part. Rather, slicing off her breast was slicing and digging into her wholeness. Of *course* she waited, procrastinated, and denied; she was unable to conceive of such a violation of her body.

SADNESS AND PAIN

The tragedy of curing a woman of breast cancer but having her life devastated by the physical or emotional effect of the cancer or its treatment occurs far too commonly. Our society has made the breast a focus of aesthetics and affection.
—Gaskin et al. 1991, 1067

Those women who use avoidance and capitulation, rather than "confrontive" coping strategies, are more emotionally distressed in the early rehabilitation stages following mastectomy than are women who deal more directly with the stress.
—Holland and Rowland 1987, 637

Anxiety, fear, and depression are documented among the majority of patients in most studies, with fear being one of the greatest disrupters of quality of life.
—Gaskin et al. 1991, 1067

What might it feel like, the first time a woman looks down on her flattened chest? What might it feel like to have others' eyes rest on the scar where a breast once rose? Like the uniqueness of our bodies and how we live with and in them, the fictional accounts here are distinct and various. No one lives through mastectomy exactly the same, and "no one told her / the worst betrayal is when / your own body / turns on you" (Harris 1988, 25).

Bobbie Ann Mason's *Spence + Lila* (1988) portrays a Kentucky farm woman, Lila, who has been married for forty years to Spence.

What sent her to the doctor were dizzy spells, but during that investigation, a "knot" was discovered:

> She felt that lump weeks ago, but she didn't mention it then. . . . The knot did feel unusual, like a piece of gristle. . . . Lila never examined her breasts the way they said to do, because her breasts were always full of lumps anyway. . . . she cannot expect to find a little knot. Spence says her breasts are like cow bags. He has funny names for them, like the affectionate names he had for his cows. . . . Names like Daisy and Bossy. Petunia. Primrose. It will be harder on him if she loses one of her breasts than it will be on her. Women can stand so much more than men can. (19)

Lila's knot is malignant. Her breast is removed, and her outward response is one of matter-of-factness laced with a bit of humor and at some moments, a puzzled reflection on what had occurred to her. The day after her surgery, Spence helps Lila walk down the hall in the hospital, pulling the I.V. pole behind her, with Lila lightly joking about her lost breast. "I didn't realize how you depend on your jugs for balance. I feel all whopper-jawed! And I have to go around holding the other one up till I can wear a brassiere" (74). Spence tries playing along, telling her he can "rig her up a sling," but at the end of the hallway she suddenly turns to him and asks, "Why do you suppose this happened to me?" "No reason," Spence replies. "Things just happen. What do you mean?" Lila muses, "I don't know. It just don't seem right" (74).

Earlier after she had received the news of her breast mass, Lila had started wondering then, too, why cancer had seemingly singled out her. Talking before surgery with her two daughters, Lila ironically noted that she "raised three younguns" on her "big jugs" and she "guess they're give out now" (30). But she does not say what she's feeling—"that the last thing she would have expected was to be attacked by disease in the very place she felt strongest. It seemed to suggest some basic failing, like the rotten core of a dying tree" (30).

"You've always been so proud of those," Lila's daughter says, touching the top of Lila's breast" (30). Postoperatively her surgeon, who really knows little about Lila other than what is on her chart, dismisses her body in (perhaps) an attempt to help her focus on her life instead of her illness: "You couldn't live without a head, or a liver, or a heart. . . . But you can live without a breast. You'll be surprised." Wise Lila, whose body and self cannot be so neatly divided, retorts, "It would be like living without balls. . . . You'd find that surprising too, but you could probably get along without them" (62).

Of course she can live without her breast, but doing so will take some time. Lila is self-conscious about the "emptiness" on her right front. She "pulls at the hospital gown, filling it out with air so she won't appear so lopsided" (81). With the drainage bottle taped to her stomach close to her shaved groin "flapping as she walks down the hall" along with her flattened chest, "she might have had a sex-change operation" (81). But in the next moment, Lila likens mastectomy to giving birth: "Part of her that used to bulge out is now vacant, the familiar growth gone. It's an empty sensation" (82). She flashes back to the recovery room when she woke up wondering what they did with the breast they cut off:

> Did it all come out in one hunk, or did they hack it out? She thought about dressing a chicken, the way she cut out the extra fat and pulled out the entrails. She thought of how it was so easy to rip raw chicken breast. (113)

But regardless of how the breast came off or what they did with the breast tissue, Lila and other women like her all must look at their incision for the first time. "Lila doesn't want to look, but she glimpses a brown spot. She wonders if they saved her nipple. . . . The brown spot is far off center" (72).

Effort should be made to help the patient look
at the incision before she goes home.
                    —Scherer 1991, 703

If a patient is uncomfortable about the appear-
ance of the operative site, problems may arise.
            —Brunner and Suddarth 1992, 1309

Audre Lorde's acclaimed *The Cancer Journals* (1980) provides a different turn to a woman's meditations on her breast cancer and mastectomy. "I want to write rage but all that comes is sadness" (13), she writes. This short sentence illuminates the complexities of a woman's response to losing a breast, and the existence of multiple, conflicting responses as she lives through the experience and beyond. Examining her chest the first time after surgery, she writes:

I looked down at the surgical area as he changed the dressing, expecting it to look like the ravaged and pitted battlefield of some major catastrophic war. But all I saw was my same soft brown skin, a little tender-looking and puffy from the middle of my chest up into my armpit, where a thin line ran. . . . The skin looked smooth and tender and untroubled. . . . It was otherwise quite unremarkable, except for the absence of that beloved swelling I had come so to love over 44 years. (44–45)

Often a kaleidoscope of emotions, different but patterned, Lorde's journal is a chronicle of the daily life that does "not forget cancer for very long, ever" a fact of her existence that keeps her armed and on her toes, "but also with a slight background noise of fear" (14).

Looking back on the early days after her surgery, Lorde describes with directness and vulnerability her fear, sorrow, and at times, resignation:

I want to write of the pain I am feeling right now, of the lukewarm tears that will not stop coming into my eyes—for what? For my lost breast? For the lost me? And which me was that again anyway? For the death I don't know how to postpone? Or how to meet elegantly? . . . I'm so tired of all this. I want to be the person I used to be, the real me. I feel sometimes that it's all a dream and surely I'm about to wake up now. (24–25)

Lorde's self-conscious reflection on the meaning of losing her breast is a startling contrast to the approach to postmastectomy "adjustment" in United States culture. Not wanting to obscure the pain, fear, and sorrow surrounding the loss of a breast she loved, to let these emotions "fossilize into yet another silence, nor to rob [her] of whatever strength can lie at the core of this experience" (9), she decides to acknowledge and examine her emotions openly. If she resists or tries to stop the pain, "it will detonate inside me, shatter me, splatter me, splatter my pieces against every wall and person" that she touches (12). Later, we will examine how Lorde's reflectiveness on her pain and sadness at this crucial point led her to reclaim herself and her body image by living what she called a more fully considered life.

So far, most of the women's lives portrayed here have explicitly or implicitly included an intimate companion: Lila's husband

Spence, Grace's husband Ben, Audre's partner Frances. Katrina Middleton's poem "Mastectomy" offers the reflection of a seventy-year-old woman whose breasts, now "wrinkled and sagged," are "no lover's fruit," nor have they been for twenty years. But like her hand or foot, her breast was *hers,* and she mourns the loss acutely, too, even though she does not foresee the added burden of worrying or wondering about a lover's response to her body as some women do. But still, she asks her doctor (who cannot hear her question), "Why couldn't you erase / the alien growth with those fancy silver tools / yet leave the flesh?" (39). Everything else that matters has left her too—a husband who died, three grown daughters, each upon her departure leaving the woman more alone, less whole, as if they took pieces of her as they left. As she looks down on her incision, what she sees are "black crosshatched threads," leaving her, as her family did, with "one more scar" (39).

Middleton's poem reminds us of the pain and sadness that breast cancer and mastectomy may evoke regardless of age, regardless of the presence or absence of a lover. The amputation of a body part, here a breast, whether young and firm or "wrinkled and sagged," brings forth a painful reassessment of one's life that, according to Lorde, is shared by women in our culture who undergo mastectomy. Part of that assessment may indeed include an intimate relationship, but it may also be heavily focused on the *totality* of one's life, loving, work, and mortality. Middleton's poem tells us that to equate a woman's postmastectomy pain and sadness merely with her apprehension of how intimate others will respond to her body (thus ignoring or dismissing the pain of women without partners or celibate women) is a cruel repudiation of the depth and breadth of the complex, multilayered experience for many women.

SHAME THROUGH OTHERS' EYES

Some women fear revulsion by their partners so much that they actually set up a self-fulfilling prophecy by refusing to exhibit themselves or make love.
                        —*Schain 1978, 472*

Patients who have not dealt physically with their own mastectomies certainly have not been able to confront their own psychological issues.
        —*Snyderman and Snyderman 1987, 534*

Reconstructive surgery may be psychologically
essential to restore self-esteem, which may
have been diminished from the mastectomy.
                              —Brown et al. 1991, 1062

What do the expressions in the eyes of others, their words or silences, their touching or not touching, mean to women who have undergone mastectomy?

Adrienne Rich's poem, "A Woman Dead in Her Forties" (1978b), gives us one glimpse. The narrator of the poem is a lifelong friend of a woman who has had a breast removed. The two of them, along with the women they grew up with, "are sitting / half-naked on rocks in sun / we look at each other and / are not ashamed" (53). They have taken off their blouses to bask, but the woman without her breast now has second thoughts: "This is not what you wanted / to show your scarred, deleted torso" (53). Not knowing how to respond—look or not look? words or silence?—the narrator barely glances at her friend "as if my look could scald you" (53). But it is not repulsion or fear the narrator feels for her friend's body; rather,

> I want to touch my fingers
> to where your breasts had been
> but we never did such things
>
> You hadn't thought everyone
> would look so perfect
> unmutilated
> you pull on
> your blouse again: stern statement:
>
> *There are things I will not share*
> *with everyone* (53)

As the poem unfolds, we learn of the narrator's deep, complex love for her friend over a lifetime, muted by convention and lies as they "kept in touch, untouching" (55), the narrator in a "proper marriage," her friend an "independent woman" (55). Looking back now after her friend's death, she second-guesses herself, wishing she had helped her friend fight not only her "unfair, unfashionable, unforgivable / woman's death" (56), but also the conventions dictating her friend's "irreproachable" life as a "dean of women" (56). Feeling the weight of all she did not say or do, she is "left laboring / with the secrets and the silence" (57), never telling her friend *how* she loved her, and never talking at her deathbed of her death.

Now, later, she comes to understand the muffled words, the unexpressed emotions, the averted language: "We stayed mute and disloyal / because we were afraid" (58). Coming to this awareness too late, she pledges to do things differently, honoring the dead and the living: "from here on / I want more crazy mourning, more howl, more keening" (58).

Of course there is more going on here than a woman who died of breast cancer in her forties. The poem is a woman's lament, the grief of unspoken love between two women. But it is also the illumination of a love that does not recoil from the scars of a "sliced-off breast" of a lover. The poem is, rather, an expression of a deep and remarkable love that would prompt the following act of tender acceptance: "I would have touched my fingers / to where your breasts had been / but we never did such things" (58).

This woman's sorrow is a contrast to Kay Schodek's short poem "Mastectomy" (1988) where we find the voice of a woman, scarred from mastectomy, comparing her body to a mummy's. Her loss is larger, it seems, than that of the mummy, which retains even in death fleshy remnants, markers of life, reminders of the body/self, former sites of intimacy, the dailiness of touch. Her story is enlarged by the mummy metaphor of death and decay she invokes for her body, the image of pyramids for breasts, and the Nile water, symbolizing breast milk and life, that continues "to curve around the pyramids." But here, in the landscape of this woman's body, her "terrain's dry / and flat as baked clay" (40).

But if a woman's own sorrow about her lost breast is not enough, some must endure the insensitivity of their health caregivers who, though perhaps well-intentioned, dismiss the profound pain of a woman who has undergone mastectomy with a flippant attempt at humor. In Jana Harris's poem, "The Lump The Swelling The Possibility of Cancer: Notes from the Oncology Clinic" (1988), a doctor airily makes conversation with a woman whose body he paints "after lighting her / up on the inside to / see where her body / went wrong" (27). We do not know the reason he postures this way (to distance himself? to ease her fear?), but his breezy joking with the silent (terrified/resigned/sad) woman takes the following form:

> He
> draws red stitch
> marks on her throat
> don't worry
> about scars, he says,
> we'll have you
> sewn up and ready
> for a Cosmopolitan
> younger man/older woman
> affair in no time,
> dontchaknow? (28)

One can speculate what a similar situation reversing the gender of doctor and patient might mean to a man fighting testicular cancer and who has had his testicles cut off: his doctor, a woman, telling him he will be ready for the Chippendales in no time. How offensive and shameful, and how sadly ridiculous the victim of such misguided humor must feel. Such insensitive verbal swaggering in the presence of vulnerable, frightened patients, even in the name of humor, is a behavior on which all health caregivers might self-reflect.

A final window on shame—here, its absence—is provided by Barbara Rosenblum, who described the profound changes in her body and the responses of her lover Sandy to those changes in their memoir, *Cancer in Two Voices* (1991). Like Audre Lorde, who wrote that "a lifetime of loving women had taught me that when women love each other, physical change does not alter that love" (56), Barbara found Sandy's responses loving, constant, tender, and changed only to the extent of Barbara's moods and desires. Barbara, fighting a cancer of the breast that had already begun metastatic processes throughout her body, wrote of living in her "unstable" body and living in relation to Sandy. Her writing, while infused with quiet, matter-of-fact sadness without self-pity, is full of the pain of chemotherapy, fatigue, losing her hair and her period. Losing her pubic hair was also very difficult, which made her feel "naked and embarrassed, like a prepubescent child. [She] was too exposed and didn't want to be touched" (135). Later she found that she had stopped lubricating when she became sexually aroused. That, coupled with the loss of her period, made her confused about her feelings of sexiness and sensuality.

Her portrayal of Sandy's responses to her during this devastating period in her life is one of extraordinary tenderness and acceptance. When they stopped making love in the ways they had before, their "hands found new ways to console each other" (136). And while losing a breast did alter her body image, she "never felt a diminishment of [her] femininity," because her breasts had never been the center of her womanness (138). Not so for all women, she found. Relating her experiences in a support group, she wrote of two women, one whose husband left her until her breast was reconstructed because he could not bear the sight of her; another who never got undressed in front of her husband, and when they made love, she wore her bra with prosthesis. Both accounts echo Zona Gale's poem "Jonesie," where

> home different
> he hasn't touched me
> since surgery
> refuses to discuss it
> or counseling (1988, 49)

Barbara, incredulous with the thought of someone abandoning a woman because she has one breast instead of two, wrote of her very different experience:

> I'm very lucky. Sandy has been exceptionally steadfast and easy about the changes in my body. She did not compel me to pay attention to her needs, her anxieties, her worries. She never made me feel inadequate or freakish. Her face never revealed shock or terror. She was easy with my scar, touching it delicately. . . . She was always softly, gently there, through everything. (1991, 138)

TRANSCENDENCE

The patient who aggressively seeks to control
her disease is able, in some way, to have an
influence on the course of the disease.
  —Snyderman and Snyderman 1987, 532

Women who have a sense of control over
events, actively taking a role in rehabilitation,

have been found to do better than those with a
helpless outlook.
                    —Holland and Rowland 1987, 637

How does a woman move beyond the pain, fear, anger, and sadness wrought by breast cancer and mastectomy? The journey to self-
acceptance must surely be experienced uniquely by every woman,
but the emotional travels of three woman portrayed here in poetry
and memoir help our always partial understanding of how this may
be achieved.

Patricia Goedicke's "In the Hospital" (1988) is a dreamy, delicate poem brimming with hope, transcendence, and strength. In
eight couplets, the narrator tells us how she overcame the terror and
pain of mastectomy. Within the first line of each couplet, a negative,
fatalistic image appears, and is countered with a positive, life-
affirming impression in the second:

> When they knocked me out on the operating table
> I dreamed I was flying
>
> ....
> When they were about to drown me
> I floated
>
> ....
> When they laid harsh hands on me
> I thought of fireworks I had seen with you (2)

Of course, this woman does not arrive at acceptance of what is happening to her by glib or rote recitations that deny the pain and
harshness of mastectomy. But each attempt to transcend the emotional and medical invasiveness of mastectomy—the knives, the
anesthesia, the questions, the looks, the prognosis—moves her one
step closer to a new start with her new life. And it seems with the
comfort of believing that her partner's love would be unchanged by
this crisis, she is able to do what she must with courage and con-
viction that she will survive, so much that

> When they took off my right breast
> I gave it to them. (2)

This woman is not a victim.

Nor is Audre Lorde. In her memoir, a form that is "autobiography with a vengeance" (Quinby, 1992), Lorde shows readers how her unique recovery proceeded and how she was able to overcome the pain and sadness of losing her "precious breast." One important outgrowth of Lorde's confrontation with her disease through the lenses of a black lesbian feminist is her vehement rejection of prosthesis and breast reconstruction. Lorde came to the realization that for her the speedy emphasis on wearing a prosthesis would be a sure route to avoiding the sadness, pain, and loss of separation from her breast, thereby denying her access to her own strength. She acknowledges that the feelings of "wanting to go back, of not wanting to persevere through this experience to whatever enlightenment might be at the core of it" (55) is a seductive lure to women in pain and fear of how others will respond to their changed bodies. But, she maintains, the quick fix of prosthesis encourages a nostalgic pretense of going back to one's former physical and psychic self:

> In the critical and vulnerable period following surgery, self-examination and self-evaluation are positive steps. To imply to a woman that yes, she can be the "same" as before surgery, with the skillful application of a little puff of lambswool and/or silicone gel, is to place an emphasis upon prosthesis which encourages her not to deal with herself as physically and emotionally real, even though altered and traumatized. This emphasis upon the cosmetic after surgery reinforces this society's stereotype of women, that we are only what we look or appear, so this is the only aspect of our existence we need to address. Any woman who has had a breast removed because of cancer knows she does not feel the same. But we are allowed no psychic time or space to examine what our true feelings are, to make them our own. With quick cosmetic reassurance, we are told that our feelings are not important, our appearance is all, the sum total of self. (56–57)

Thus, Lorde calls herself a warrior, a woman willing to stand up to a culture that values a woman's appearance over her health. The transcendence she experiences emerges from a brave confrontation with her life: her work; her relationships; and her questioning of values, such as how to spend her time and energy, and how to challenge structures that support external and destructive controls over women's lives.

In other words, Lorde's transcendence of the disease and amputation was the result of her learning to live a more fully considered life, an ability that "grows and deepens as one faces one's own mortality" (57). Prostheses and reconstruction, according to Lorde, attempt to sidestep self-reflection and scrutiny of one's life. They keep women "in a position of perpetual and secret insufficiency, infantilized and dependent for her identity upon an external definition by appearance" (58). By refusing to limit her loss to the physical, she was able to move into the "terrible" meaning of living and dying. "After all," she writes, "what could we possibly be afraid of after having admitted to ourselves that we had dealt face to face with death and not embraced it?" (53).

Likewise, Deena Metzger's "I Am No Longer Afraid" (1988), is jubilant and defiant, and celebrates the poet's arrival at transcendence. This sphere is a place she inhabits because she, like Lorde, is a warrior, but a gentle one "who does not kill or wound" (71). Throughout the piece she recalls images of her Amazon sisters, and finds in her scar the earthy, majestic strength of trees. What used to be a "fine red line" across her chest now has a branch that winds around it:

> Green leaves cover the branch, grapes hang there and a bird
>   appears.
> What grows in me now is vital and does not cause me harm.
>   I think the bird is singing. (71)

Referring back to the unseen destruction cancer did beneath her skin, she now sees life-giving vitality—the branch is covered with green leaves and grapes, and a singing bird appears. As she relinquishes some of the scars, she invents herself with the "care given to an illuminated manuscript" (71); on her chest—the "book of my body"—she has "permanently inscribed a tree" (71). Now her strength is joyous and determined, but we think this battle must have been hard fought, and that her transcendence was not speedy and neat. While she is "no longer ashamed to make love," we assume she once was; now "love is a battle I / can win" (71). By placing the words love and battle together, along with using the present instead of the past tense, she may be addressing her continuing challenge to ward off self-doubt and fear in order to love herself again, and clearly, she is winning.

"Cancer is a conjuring word," wrote Janis Coombs Epps (1990), herself a survivor of it. That is what these poems and stories tell us too, that in addition to the confrontations with death that cancer evokes, the added turn of breasts as a dimension of many women's sexual selves makes the disease more difficult, confrontive, and terrifying than it would be otherwise. Even hearing the words disturbs most women, unable to conceive what it might be like to have their breasts cut off.

The poems and stories also tell us how subjectively experienced breast cancer is, really like all disease. In spite of all the protocols, treatment plans, and counseling techniques developed for women who have undergone mastectomy, there are no ready-made answers or predictability to how an individual woman will experience mastectomy. Anatole Broyard, a writer who had prostate cancer and died from it, made an observation that, along with these poems and stories, may help us remember the intensely personal lived experience of any illness: "If I were to demystify or deconstruct my cancer, I might find that there is no absolute diagnosis, no single agreed-upon text, but only the interpretation each . . . patient makes" (1992, 21).

One possible amendment. Perhaps there *is* some predictability regarding how a woman might experience breast cancer and mastectomy. Audre Lorde reminds us

each woman responds to the crisis that [breast] cancer brings to her life out of a whole pattern, which is the design of who she is and how her life has been lived. The weave of her everyday existence is the training ground for how she handles crisis. (1980, 9)

Louise Dahl-Wolfe (American, 1896-1989). *Colette*, 1951. Gelatin silver print, 10⅞ × 13⅛ in. The National Museum of Women in the Arts. Gift of Helen Cuming Ziegler.

Chapter 4

Menopause

Although widely thought to be "normal" aging, menopause should not be considered harmless; it is associated with a number of potentially adverse changes, including acceleration of age-related bone loss, increase in the risk of coronary heart disease, changes in the reproductive organs (particularly thinning and atrophy of the vaginal and urethral mucosa), and hot flushes.

—Kelley 1989, 2585

We live in a patriarchy that deeply influences the way we think and feel about our gendered selves. This same culture is ageist and consumerist, a combination that in the context of patriarchy situates women as most valuable when they are young, thin, firm—that is, in a body swimming in estrogen. The message is relentless and ubiquitous: stay young, stay thin, stay attractive. We find the message on the streets, in our offices and schools (even medical schools), in every possible media from billboards to films to magazines to television: you are valued and valuable when you are young and thin and able to reproduce. Ursula K. LeGuin observes it this way:

The menopause is probably the least glamorous topic imaginable; and this is interesting, because it is one of the very few topics of which cling some shreds and remnants of taboo. A serious mention of menopause is usually met with uneasy silence; a sneering reference to it is usually met with relieved sniggers. Both the silence and the sniggering are pretty sure indications of taboo. (1989, 3)

Thus, it is not surprising that in twentieth-century United States culture, menopause is thought of as a deficiency disease, not a natural event. One of the most widely read medical textbooks, and eleventh edition of *Harrison's Principles of Internal Medicine* (Braunwald 1987), describes menopause in this way:

> The menopause is defined as the final episode of menstrual bleeding in women. . . . During this period there is a gradual but progressive loss of ovarian function and a variety of endocrine, somatic, and psychological changes. . . . The most common menopausal symptoms are those of vasomotor instability (hot flush), atrophy of the urogenital epithelium and skin, decreased size of the breasts, and osteoporosis. Approximately 40% of women in the postmenopausal period develop symptoms serious enough to seek medical assistance. . . . The decrease in size of the organs of the female reproductive tract and breasts during the menopause is the consequence of estrogen deficiency. The endometrium becomes thin and atrophic in most . . . and the vaginal mucosa and urethra also become thin and atrophic. . . . Other symptoms commonly associated with the hot flush, including nervousness, anxiety, irritability, and depression, may or may not be due to estrogen deficiency. (1822–24)

Of course the language is medical—the intended reader is a physician. Thus the focus is impersonal and highly clinical, precisely how Western medicine has evolved in this century. The object of inquiry is a significantly abstracted member of the category Woman, specifically Menopausal Woman. She is not distinctive, singular, or exceptional. Moreover, when we examine the words used to describe physiological dimensions of Menopausal Woman, we find words denoting scarcity and inadequacy: final, loss, instability, atrophy, decreased size, deficiency, nervousness, anxiety, irritability, depression.

But if that were not enough—this portrait of Menopausal Woman as one with dry vagina and sagging breasts—we have to contend with psychosocial portraits that further fix and deepen beliefs about the ill effects of menopause already well in place by a patriarchic popular culture. A particularly troubling account appears in the ninth edition of *Obstetrics and Gynecology* (Willson and Carrington 1991b). After a lengthy discussion of the physiological basis of menopause and its clinical manifestations, the author describes other symptoms that often accompany menopause:

> Headache, insomnia, vertigo, depression, and feelings of hopelessness, worthlessness, and self-condemnation are often experienced during the climacteric. . . . Few women understand the physiologic changes that occur during climacteric. . . . Many have bizarre ideas of what to expect. Their fears include obesity, excessive hair growth, and other changes in their bodies that will make them less attractive; loss of sexual appetite; the development of psychoses; and, of course, the undeniable fact that they are getting old. (Willson, 622)

But what is even more insidious is the following universalizing account of menopausal or postmenopausal women in that same *current* text:

> Many women who have been busy caring for their families find that their children no longer need them and their husbands are preoccupied with their jobs. These women have less and less to do, and too few know how to make use of the many free hours available to them. Those who are working may realize that there is no hope of advancing to more interesting or responsible positions. (Willson, 622)

Disturbing is not only their essentializing distortions of the hugely varied experiences of women, but also their insinuations that Menopausal Woman defines herself almost entirely in terms of her role as wife/mother. Willson adds the final frame to this extraordinarily facile image of Menopausal Woman by stating, "No woman can blithely disregard the change in her appearance and the prospect of progressive aging" (623).

What does imaginative literature tell us about this deficiency state? The messages are quite different from the medicalized accounts. In fact, one reading both accounts may wonder if the same phenomenon is portrayed in each. Certainly the imaginative writers attend to many similar feelings described by the medical writers. However, the language used, and the contexts and particularities of the former make each woman's lived experience of menopause more abundant, more layered, and lived within a far greater range of emotional response that those suggested by the more "objectified" accounts. Christine Downing's (1991) disclosure characterizes some of these discursive differences:

> I don't want to get around it. I want to live it. I don't want to "treat" it or "cure" it, though I do want to honor it with curiosity and with therapy (therapia), attention of the kind one devotes to sacred mysteries. I want menopause to be a soul event, which means letting it be transformative. (np)

The sketches of menopause we selected portray several women's individual, deeply personal, and idiosyncratic response to this significant change in their lives. As we read their words, we began to hear different but recurring strains to a universal event for women. Not intended to be exhaustive or representative, these are situated accounts of several women experiencing menopause. As such, they may deepen and enlarge our understanding of menopause while challenging some of the myths and the misogyny that exist in our culture regarding menopause.

URGENCY

Supportive therapy, especially when the woman is greatly distressed, is most helpful. . . . If it is decided that the problem is not menopausal, psychiatric referral is often more accepted by the patient than if suggested by her own general practitioner. . . . Tranquilizers and hypnotics are frequently prescribed at the time of menopause.
> —McEwan 1985, 160

One literary portrayal of menopause is a sense of urgency. The cessation of a monthly ritual that has been a deeply integral part of a woman's life and identity may cause her to think about its symbolic significance in her life span. While menopause may be thought of as a rite, passage, or beginning, it is also the *end* of one significant dimension of a woman's life. Thus it may prompt an uneasy examination of the ratio of time remaining to unrealized dreams. In Carla Kandinsky's (1991) poem, "As a Woman Grows Older," we find an unrestrained appraisal of what one particular woman finds she has not experienced. She now finds that "all the things / you've missed you crave"; this seemingly random list includes "a Japanese / lover, learning to say fuck in Greek, / a week in Spain" (30). Similarly, looking back at lapses in her experiences, she begins to wonder about choices she made that now seem to have been made unreflectively, even unconsciously. Why, she wonders, has she always lived in the East Bay, never in San Francisco? Why does she now want an emerald instead of her jade? Why does she crave bacon, pork chops, and steak after years of vegetarianism? Why does she find that now "desire / either sleeps for weeks or reaches / out to grab you with merciless claws / rattling your teeth" (30)? She tells us why in the last few lines of the poem:

> At times you reach out and grab
> you try to have it this time around,
> just in case there's no reincarnation.
> Just in case when the blood stops
> flowing it really is the end. (30)

Of course menopause is not "the end," but the symbolic significance of the end of the monthly flow of blood so rich in possibility forces her to take a meditative look at the choices and decisions she has made, and those yet to be made, now more conscious of time than before.

This sense of urgency may be confused with depression by those who have been led to believe that the latter is a fairly predictable response to menopause. Examination of one's life—looking ahead and behind with an eye on the calendar—is not pathological, but may be interpreted as such by those who have allowed menopause to be medicalized, and those who have been seduced by our culture's canonization of youth. For women to experience menopause more existentially than physically is indeed a puzzling thought, but is one that women may relate to more fully if they were released from prescriptive medical renderings of menopause.

SOMETHING SIGNIFICANT IS HAPPENING

*The large number of ovarian follicles with
which a woman is born progressively declines
throughout her lifetime. All through childhood,
adolescence, and maturity, the follicles are lost
by ovulation and atresia. Eventually, the total
number is almost exhausted, and the ovarian
hormone secretion diminishes. The decreased
ovarian estrogen produced by the few follicles
that are left is insufficient to inhibit the pitu-
itary gonadotropins, and FSH and LH levels
greatly increase. When the level of ovarian es-
trogens falls below a certain critical amount,
the hypothalamic-pituitary-ovarian feedback
system is altered and cycles stop.*
                                        —*Sloane 1985, 490–91*

Such urgent examination of what is left may be tied to a melancholic or sentimental look backward to the lived experience of
menstruation so much a part of a woman's life that it was as natural
as breathing, noticed only when it became difficult, as when one is
in the presence of thin air. Lucille Clifton's (1991a) poem, "to my
last period," is one such poem. Here she familiarizes her period, giving it life affectionately as "girl," but a girl who never appeared
without trouble, "splendid in your red dress" (267). Yet even with
the "trouble" (pain? unexpected appearances?), she now thinks differently as the "girl" begins to leave. The poem's voice calls forth
images of huddled grandmothers who "after the hussy has gone / sit
holding her photograph / and sighing, *wasn't she / beautiful?
wasn't she beautiful?*" (267).

But what did these grandmothers mean, "beautiful"? Why
does the poet choose the slightly juxtaposed image of a now beautiful hussy to portray the former appearance of blood? Most likely it
is the ambivalence many women feel toward menstruation—the
lived experience of pain and bloating, contrasted with its earthy,
rich, symbolic nature, perhaps felt more acutely at menstruation's
cessation.

Janet McCann's (1991) poem, "Forty-five," presents a more
melancholic examination of menopause. Driving with her five-year-
old son, her "last one," the woman describes their conversation
about sunsets. Looking at his upturned face beside her "in the early

chill," she finds an "ache like a cloud / an old pain / that will not articulate / that will not say itself" (144). This deep ache is felt not in moments of solitude or loneliness, but at a time of literal connection with her child, a tangible flesh made possible by this very blood flow now ending. Walking into the house after the car ride, mother and son are hand in hand, and the vague feeling lingers: "my body hangs on me / like an old dress" (144). Something—a way of being, a seemingly inseparable component of our identity—is leaving or missing, and one of the physical reminders of its former presence may be those we love most deeply, namely, our children. The musings of this woman have a different sound from the earlier clinical account that "no woman can blithely disregard the change in her appearance and the prospect of progressive aging." Of course the aging described here is not blithely ignored. Rather, it is thoughtfully and yes, sadly considered, but with a more reflective, authentic consideration than the cosmetic superficiality implied by the clinical description.

Joanne Seltzer (1991) describes her menopausal transition in a much less somber way in "No More Xs on my Calendar, No More PMS." Using imagery similar to Clifton, she calls her period a "ruby-colored friend" who had "visited" her (25). Now, without these monthly visits, she does not miss her friend or think of her, with one wry exception: "once in a blue moon / when the sun defers / to the power of light / leaving me nothing / to howl about" (25). This howling, from the murmuring sounds of women gathered at our various twentieth-century wells to the roar of women outraged at the pharmaceutical and surgical management of our bodies, situates us with other women in a connective gendered web, so that talking to another woman is sometimes the only thing that comforts us. Or as Trudy Riley describes these experiences: "I am deep into a litany of complaints that I know she will understand" (1991, 140).

A RITE, A RELIEF

Menopause is often identified with depression.
It has been observed that treating patients in
the immediate postmenopausal period with
estrogen replacement therapy stops the flushes,

flashes, insomnia, and night sweats. With a
good night's rest, the patient often loses her
depression, fatigue, irritability, and headaches.
                        —Barber 1988, 272–73

What about the freedom menopause brings to women? What about the women who proceed through menopause with few physical symptoms, and those who actually look forward to it as more than reproductive release but as a joyful transition into a more fully lived life?

Marge Piercy's poem, "Something to Look Forward To," is an earthly reflection on menstruation and a sardonic projection of how she will respond to its end. In reflective moments on the appearance of blood, the narrator writes:

> When my womb opens its lips on the full
> of dark of the moon, that connection
> aligns me as it does the sea. I quiver,
> a compass needle thrilling with magnetism. (1988, 26)

But for each moment of connection, for every celebration, there is a dark side to this monthly ritual: "the trail of red amoebae / crawling onto hostess' sheets to signal my body's disregard of calendar, clock" (26), or during a panel with "four males / I the token woman and they with iron bladders" when she felt "that wetness and wanted to strangle / my womb like a mouse" (27). For now, deep into the menstrual pain—"demon crab claws / gouging my belly" (14)—she describes how she will celebrate menopause:

> I will secretly dance
> and pour out a cup of wine on the earth
> when time stops that leak permanently;
> I will burn my last tampons as votive candles. (27)

Which is to say that in the midst of demon crab claws, many women project relief and release when those crabs will no longer gouge. Like the twelve-year-old Penny in the poem who, "being handed a napkin / the size of an ironing board cover, cried out / Do I have to do this from now till I die?" (27), these literary women often eagerly anticipate middle age when it will stop: "Good, said Penny, there's something to look forward to" (27). As with Clifton's grandmothers, the menstrual hussy just *may* become beautiful—but only when she is gone.

HYSTERECTOMY

Among the 156 women undergoing hysterec-
tomy . . . 30 had bilateral oophorectomies. . . .
Among these bilaterally oophorectomized
women, there was no evidence of an excess of
psychiatric morbidity (compared to non-
oophorectomized women). . . . It seems likely
that the psychiatric outcome is no worse after
hysterectomy combined with oophorectomy,
than after oophorectomy alone.
—Gath and Rose 1985, 37

Almost a cliché: the ubiquitous hysterectomy. So tied to women's reproductivity, the uterus becomes easy for others—physicians, husbands, lovers, children—to discount or trivialize, or literally and figuratively throw away once childbearing is over. Hysterectomy is similar to but distinctly different from menopause; variables to how it is experienced are many, including age, the presence or absence of children, or if the ovaries are removed. This abrupt removal of the uterus is different from the often slow, sometimes lazy transition of menopause when symptoms surface, then go underground, then resurface sluggishly or with a vengeance. Hysterectomy forces a quick burial with too little time to mourn and grieve, with no ritual passage like that afforded by menopause.

Because an important dimension of one's sexual identity is actually removed, the metaphorical thought that hysterectomy rouses is different from those a natural menopause evokes. In Gail Koplow's (1991) "Eggs," a twelve-year-old girl waves to her mother at the window in the hospital where she is having a hysterectomy. The daughter weeps silently, and knows that someday she will ask her mother "if she minded, if her heart hurt when they took the eggs. . . . What happens to a woman's soul when leggy flesh emerges from her own? I want to ask. What knife cuts deeper, tell me, or what sensuality surpasses birth?" (145). Later, the daughter, now a woman nearing menopause, thinks again about those eggs—her own eggs, all women's eggs, and again her mother's eggs:

It's eggs I've always had a passion for, amazement, yearning, at the tumbling down of eggs, miraculous, I've seen them born, those fabulous haphazard eggs. And maybe then her eyes would fill. She'd take my hand at last and say, not everyone talks. (146)

Lucille Clifton's (1991b) "poem to my uterus" portrays a similar intimate relationship a woman has with her uterus. Her uterus has been "patient / as a sock / while i have slippered into you / my-dead and living children" (175). But it is much more, a living site or her *cyclic* life: her "bloody print"; an earthy source of one dimension of her *woman's* life: her "estrogen kitchen"; a darkly mysterious dwelling of her *sexual* life: her "black bag of desire" (175). When this sock is cut out, she wonders:

> where can i go
> barefoot
> without you?
> where can you go
> without me? (175)

What happens, then, to a woman abruptly facing herself without this part of her that has been deeply enmeshed in her identity?

Lynne Sharon Schwartz's (1987) story, "So You're Going to Have a New Body!," is one woman's lived experience of hysterectomy that has not been easy, routinized, or textbook-predictable. Her talks to herself, her physician, her family, and her lover are laced with cynicism, fear, uncertainty, and sadness in a story both humorous and bitter. Much of her early cynicism is directed toward her well-meaning but insensitive physician who consoles her with clichéd talks about "feeling like a new person in six weeks," not to worry about the scar "no one can see," and "fixing" lingering symptoms with hormones. He even trivializes what she has thought and felt but not said, that somehow there is a link between her uterus and her femininity, noting that she is "much too intelligent . . . for that" (42).

One of the most troubling concerns of the woman is the decision to remove her ovaries or not. In her confused and vulnerable state, her doctor offers the following breezy yet manipulative advice:

> The decision is entirely up to you. However, I like to take the ovaries out whenever I can, as long as I'm in there. That way there is no danger of ovarian cancer, which strikes one in a hundred women in your age group. There is really nothing you need ovaries for. You have had three children and don't intend to have any more. Ovarian cancer is incurable and a terrible

death. I've seen women your age. . . . However, the decision is entirely up to you. (43)

She thinks: "No, for with the same logic he could cut off my head to avert a brain tumor" (43). Yet when questioned by her doctor again immediately before the operation in her Demerol haze, she says "Take them, they're yours" (44).

In her postoperative office visit, her physician is not suddenly struck with sensitivity. As she practices indifference with her feet in the stirrups, the doctor says she may resume most "normal activities." Her recuperation becomes a roller coaster ride, full of fatigue, tears, and wonder at her new body's appearance (thinner ankles because of no fluid retention: "an unexpected plus"), and her new body's "strange responses to [her] husband's embraces" (53). Since she finds herself with questions she cannot ask her doctor or husband, her restlessness, uncertainty, and insecurity about the changes in herself lead her to call an old friend and sometimes-lover (a physician himself), who happily agrees to help her "overcome the mystery of the sexual stranger" in her new body. And that he does as she rediscovers herself "buried deep, deep in the crevices of hidden tissues and disconnected circuits," which will, she feels certain, "emerge again and replace the imposter in the conjugal bed" (54).

Yet, in spite of the familiar pleasure she experiences with her lover, she asks him what many women must wonder after a hysterectomy: "Do I feel any different inside?" After exquisitely describing how she *does* feel, he plunges into a physiological description, which sounds much like an abstracted clinical description, unaware of the horrified ears upon which these words fall:

He explains that in the absence of the cervix, which is the opening of the uterus, the back wall of the vagina is sewn up so that in effect what you have there now is a dead end. As he explains, it seems obvious and inevitable, but strange to say, you have never figured this out before or even thought about it. (It is something your doctor neglected to mention.) Nor have you poked around on your own, having preferred to remain ignorant. So it is rather a shock, this realization that you have a dead end. You always imagined yourself, along with all women, as having an easy passage from inside to out, a constant trafficking between the heart of the world and the heart of yourself. This was what distinguished you from men. (54)

What does Schwartz's patient tell us about how hysterectomy may be lived? She tells us that while the body has wondrous capacities to mend itself with precision and predictability, healing oneself is quite another matter.

She is much like the woman in Melanie Kaye/Kantrowitz's (1991) poem "eyes," who has had enough of cancer and refuses to take estrogen, even knowing what its lack is doing to her body. Similar to the clinical descriptions of the "thinning and atrophy of the vaginal mucosa," the narrator's description of her own vagina is that "it's all shriveled." Her image is reinforced when she, feet up in stirrups, is examined by a chatty RN who "sticks her hand up into [her]" and casually remarks "atrophied the tissue thins out & looks sort of shiny red / what we call little old lady's vagina" (131). Throughout the examination, the patient's lover is stroking her hair at the head of the table.

Back home, the narrator says to her lover, "See I told you," only to be rebutted as her lover places a mirror near a lamp on the floor and asks, "want to look? . . . come look / I want you to see how pretty" (132). The narrator does eventually squat over the mirror as her lover, in the next room, hears her laughingly say "oh / it IS pretty" (132).

Within these fictional portrayals of women's experiences of menopause or hysterectomy, we are better able to feel the varied textures and hear the singular expressions of women differently situated by culture, race, or sexual identities, who are nonetheless bound together by biological experiences common to many—sometimes all—women. Some of these narrative voices are quietly reflective, such as McCann's mother in "Forty-five," who recognizes her unarticulated ache in the presence of her last child. Others want to talk about it, often with other women, such as the woman in Gail Koplow's "Eggs," or the patient in Melanie Kaye/Kantrowitz's poem "eyes." Here connection is balm for sadness or confusion.

Similarly, each woman's story is uniquely hers—*kin* to the abstract universalizing clinical accounts, but often *distant* kin. That is, looking back at one's reproductive years with some melancholy, even romanticizing those years, sad that they were not lived more fully or with awareness of their inherent wonder and mystery, is *not* the same as depression. Yet such emotional response is often medicalized to resemble depression.

Nor is a woman's response to physiological changes in her body due to decreased estrogen necessarily anxiety about aging, but may be a natural response to the messages of a patriarchal, ageist culture that says to menopausal women: "Your value is low now that you possess neither the ability to reproduce nor the youthful characteristics our culture views as beautiful. Your deficiencies are psychological and physical."

Menopause, as portrayed in these few literary accounts, is a complicated, unique experience that may or may not be similarly shared by women in our culture. What these accounts *do* tell us, however, is that menopause cannot be conceived as a bloodless, abstract experience.

Elizabeth Layton (American, 1909–1993). *Self Portrait—Holding Rose With Thorns*. Pastel with pencil on paper. 18″ × 7″. The National Museum of Women in the Arts. Gift of Wallace and Wilhelmina Holladay.

Chapter 5

Aging

*Elderly women...seem to have poorer psycho-
logical functioning than their male peers; they
are more likely to suffer loneliness, anxiety, to
have weaker self concepts, and lower levels of
morale/life satisfaction.*
                                    —Taylor 1992, 25

"It's hard work," Lilly's father tells her about getting old in *The
Singing Teacher* when she finds him pouring two hefty shots of
whiskey at his best friend Bert's grave, one for him, one for the ab-
sent Bert (Skramstad 1992, 175).

"Hard work" cannot even begin to untangle the twisted, deep
roots of what it means to be old—that is, *not young*—in twentieth
century North American culture. If the physical transitions are not
enough to adjust to—the body moving differently, acting differently,
responding differently—older persons must live in an ageist culture
that often ignores, denigrates, or ghettoizes them. Barbara Macdonald (1983) boldly describes this culture's fixed portrait of aging: "Old
is ugly, old is powerless, old is the end, and therefore . . . old is what
no one could possibly want to be" (91).

While medical/nursing geriatrics texts almost always include a
section or chapter on the psychosocial dimensions of aging, such literature often appears to sidestep the psychic issues of aging by fo-

cusing on *disease* processes rather than the spiritual malaise older humans may experience as they attempt to lead meaningful lives in an ageist culture. In fact, Anderson and Williams (1989) write that the "outstanding thesis of modern geriatric medicine is that old people who are ill are unwell not because they are old but because there is some disease present" (1).

Thus, for many health professionals, aging is a disease that can be treated medically, a message they deliver explicitly and implicitly to their patients and ultimately to the marketplace. Yet a strictly medicalized response to aging is, perhaps, a disguised rejection or fear of aging, and ultimately a denial of death. The cultural clichés implicit in or arising from these clinical attempts to slow down or reverse aging reinscribe even more deeply the gold standard of youth. To the extent we ignore or deny our experience of aging, we look to magic pharmaceutical bullets or become vulnerable to what the marketplace tells us to feel and thus buy—clothing, housing, food and personal products, recreation. One repressive stereotype is replaced by another: the anxious, fearful, slow-witted old person becomes the hip young person in an old person's body. Macdonald (1983) describes this phenomena in terms of older women:

> The process of aging has been hidden from us all our lives. We are told that with the help of modern medicine and technology old age isn't really necessary. One can have an active life right up to the "end." You are as young as you think you are. There are hair dyes to make your hair look its "natural color," with creams to remove the wrinkles and brown spots, and with all of these no woman should look as though she is "failing"—she should look "well-preserved." (99)

If these cultural stereotypes are not enough, old women have another burden: living in a patriarchy that prescribes women's roles as unselfish nurturers. This role is intensified even in old age by our culture's expectations for grandmothering, another form of sorting women into assigned roles. The idea of an old woman wanting as little to do with the care of children, even her own grandchildren, is foreign, unnatural, perceived as selfish or eccentric.

In spite of this "useful" grandmothering function, Copper (1986) maintains that "older women are seen as a burden to the patriarchy, never as a threat. One of the reasons that older women are invisible is that a patriarchal culture defines female purpose as sexual or reproductive. So what are old women for?" (54). Without impugning the joy that many women experience as grandmothers, freed from the dailiness and fatigue of caring for children, we still must ask, what about those women who are not grandmothers literally or figuratively?

The following sections attempt to unravel some of these notions of old women. Our intent is not to portray a Pollyanna perspective of aging women, but rather to provide literary exemplars of women who by choice or chance defy ageist stereotypes. The literature here portrays women engaged in the unexpected, the commonly unsanctioned by contemporary North American culture: women seeking solitude, creatively working, sexual. And yes, some of the literature here does depict women struggling with their changing roles and bodies, with the conditioned cultural responses to these transformations. All of these responses are found in the following sections, which include "O Blessed Solitude," "The Enduring Spirit," and "Beyond Hags and Old Maids."

O BLESSED SOLITUDE

The disengagement theory . . . see[s] aging as an inevitable, mutual withdrawal or disengagement of the individual from society. . . . This results in decreased interaction between the aging person and others in the social system to which he belongs.
—Patrick 1986, 61

One of the many exploitive stereotypes of older women is the cheery, aproned, flushed, nourishing, storytelling, pie-baking grandmother. Grandmothering is older women's natural state, because here is where real joy and fulfillment comes from their relationships with children. Even though she is no longer reproductive or physically attractive/seductive to men, she *is* useful (and nonthreatening) as the nurturing source of unwavering strength and unconditional love.

This is not to say that many older women do not revel in the widening circles of their extended families, experiencing deep pleasure from relationships not shackled with the duties of child care.

But why, asks Cynthia Rich, are older women supposed to be interested only in "future generations and not in themselves or each other?" (Swallow 1986, 200). This is one of the questions posed by Tillie Olsen's Eva in *Tell Me a Riddle* (1956), and an issue raised in the following section: Why is the image of an older woman who wants a life of solitude, *not* caregiving/tending/rocking, *not* moving to the rhythms of others, *not* "drowning in to needing and being needed," so problematic? Why is she perceived as unnatural?

Eva, surely one of the most tragic women in literature, has been married for forty-seven years to David—years full of near poverty, the needs of seven children, David's demands, and self-sacrifice. But finally she said, "Enough. Now they had no children. . . . She would not exchange her solitude for anything. *Never again to be forced to move to the rhythms of others*" (76).

The tragedy springs from her family's childlike treatment of her, shielding her from bad news and seizing decision-making from her. While Eva's clear, repetitious desire is to live her life from within, now freed from the external labor of tending to a family, her family refuses to listen. Mired in their own needs and problems, her family casts an image of Eva that keeps her still and always moving to the rhythms of others. When they learn of her advanced cancer, they decide not to tell her and plan without her consent how she will spend her remaining time, consistently denying her a voice even in her own dying.

The theme of their decisions: the presence of her children and grandchildren would be the most meaningful way for Eva to spend her remaining time. But shudders seized Eva when they put a baby in her lap. What had happened? It was not that she had not loved her children when they were babies. Quite the opposite:

> The love—the passion of tending—had risen with the need like a torrent; and like a torrent drowned and immolated all else. But when the need was done—oh the power that was lost in the painful damning back and drying up of what still surged, but had nowhere to go. Only the thin pulsing left that could not quiet, suffering over lives one felt, but could no longer hold nor help. (92–93)

That place where she had lived and passionately loved her children was now a dry riverbed, but still, she believed, there were "springs, [and] the springs were in her seeking. . . . Somewhere coherence, transport, meaning. If they would but leave her in the air now stilled of clamor, in the reconciled solitude, to journey on" (93).

But babies and small children still tugged, pulled, nuzzled, devoured, needed: "Tell me a riddle Grandma. . . . Look Grammy. . . . Watch me, Grandma. . . . Be my nap bed, Grammy" (95). No, she said, too late, too silently, and they continued to devour. Eva literally cannot hide, even hunched deep in her granddaughter's closet. There she is found as a "trembling little body hurls itself beside her. . . . (Is this where you hide too, Grammy? It's my secret place, we have a secret now). And the sweat beads, and the long shudder seizes" (100).

If that were not enough, her own children's neediness still mined her dry spirit. Her daughter Vivi, thinking that if she spilled her memories in front of her mother, Eva would know how much the past was cherished and still lived in her children. Vivi describes her memories of Eva's endless nurturing: nursing babies, lowering hems, washing sweaters. Instead of receiving these memories as jewels to savor then or to take out later to regard with sweetness and pleasure, Eva can only think, "Stop it, daughter, stop it, leave that time" (97). But no one heard her thoughts, and "day after day, the spilling memories. Worse now, questions, too. Even the grandchildren: Grandma, in the olden days when you were little. . . ." (98).

Jim Harrison (1991) wonders: To what degree is the perception of reality consensual? Eva's family portrays the total failure of one's ability to perceive another's reality—here, Eva's—and in doing so denies her the sacred right to decide what the last of her living and the story of her dying would be.

The fictional Eva reminds us, and those who would sort women into roles they do not want, that the prescribed life denies women the essential human dimension of choosing the self. Families, lovers, friends, health caregivers, as they seek to understand and not to dictate and prescribe what is best for an older woman might think of Harrison's gentle dictum: "We should encourage ourselves to be a whale, a woman, a plant or planet, a lake, the night sky" (265). An *older* woman at that.

In her poem "A Woman Alone" (1975, 16-17), Denise Levertov provides a similar, although in this case quite celebratory, portrayal of an older woman without requisite family attachments. While we are unsure how old the "she" is in the poem, it is apparent that earlier she experienced life widely and variously, so much at this point in her life she has trouble remembering "which of two lovers it was with whom she felt / this or that moment of pleasure." But now, without her unnamed but implicit former partner, she can do what she could or would not in his/her presence:

> sit or walk for hours after a movie
> talking earnestly and with burst of laughter
> with friends, without worrying
> that it's late, dinner at midnight, her time
> spent without counting the change . . .
> When half her bed is covered with books
> and no one is kept awake by the reading light
> and she disconnects the phone, to sleep till noon.

Apparently her partner had expectations for her that now and perhaps then seemed repressive, monotonous, bloodless: eating dinner at regular times, returning home at predictable hours, lying in bed, wide awake in the dark.

Unshackled, relieved, now celebrating ("selfpity dries up, a joy untainted by guilt lifts her"), she lives more fully awake with a kind of "sober euphoria" that makes her believe in her future as an old woman, one who is a wanderer, who is "seamed and brown," and who now watches people and places without being watched. She is quietly exhilarated now, alone, working her way to being "tough and wise." And now, "she can say without shame or deceit, / O blessed solitude."

Nowhere in these lines do we find the usual appendages of many old women: that is, an aging partner, children and grandchildren. Nowhere do we see dependence, or loneliness, or weakness. Instead, the heartbeat of this poem grows stronger and steadier—at times still unsure, vulnerable but not weak. Her solitude, newly found in old age, is something she had been waiting to experience all her life.

In her *Journal of a Solitude* (1973), May Sarton describes the importance of her chosen solitude at age sixty. At her home in rural Maine, she confronts a depression by writing, resting, gardening, and tending to friends. She recognizes solitude not as a peaceful state that one easily enters, but as "that intense, hungry face at the window, starved cat, starved person. It is making space to *be there*" (57). Being there is, in part, her "real" life, difficult as it is at times:

That is what is strange—that friends, even passionate love, are not my real life unless there is time alone in which to explore and to discover what is happening or has happened. Without the interruptions, nourishing and maddening, this life would become arid. Yet I taste it fully only when I am alone here and "the house and I resume old conversations." (11)

Sarton's journal becomes, really, a journey of solitude—a journey deep into herself to unearth what she thinks and feels. Conscious of this purposeful journey, she tries not to be anxious about filling her days with activity to deflect the outward and inner silence. But her nagging fear is that she will be unable to find herself when she breaks through "into the rough rocky depths, to the matrix itself" (12).

As a sixty-year-old woman writing these words, Sarton wrote consciously of her literal aloneness. Deeply cognizant of the difficulties of many women to experience what she is able to, she writes:

It is harder for women to clear space around whatever it is they want to do beyond household chores and family life. Their lives are fragmented . . . this is the cry I get in so many letters—they cry not so much for "a room of one's own" as time of one's own. Conflict becomes acute, whatever it may be about, when there's no margin left on any day in which to try at least to resolve it. (56)

An older woman's desire for solitude may seem absurd when we consider the imposed solitary confinement and ghettoization of the old in our ageist culture. Many older persons, women and men, hunger for the human connection of a family and friends—even strangers. Still, Sarton's life is a luminary of the potential richness of a freely chosen and consciously lived inner life. Her solitude gives her the time to think, what she views as the greatest luxury in her life because it enables her "time to be." Yet she views this as a huge responsibility, too, using time well and being all she can in whatever years are left to her (40).

Vita Sackville-West's novel, *All Passion Spent* (1931), is a smoothly fluent yet crisp narrative of Lady Shane, a newly widowed woman in her eighties. All her life, from her Victorian childhood through the properly lived present, has been privileged, sheltered, and teeming with family and caregivers. When Lord Shane dies, her children consult each other singly and as a group regarding what should be "done" with their mother. They do so without seeking her input, and without having a clue about her wishes. This was not new behavior. Indeed, or so they thought, their mother

> had no will of her own; all her life long, gracious and gentle, she had been wholly submissive—an appendage. . . . That she might have ideas which she kept to herself never entered into their estimate. . . . She would be grateful to them for arranging her few remaining years (24–25).

Such were their perceptions of her, grounded in a lifetime of family experiences. They are surprised and puzzled, then, by her response to their plans for her widowhood, which include circulating among the spare bedrooms of her children. When she informs them she will live by herself, they find her independence an "outrage, almost a manifesto" (64). But she will not be cajoled or gently threatened; she had made up her mind quickly, assuredly, and by herself. She says, never dropping a stitch of her knitting, "I have considered the eyes of the world for so long that I think it is time I had a little holiday from them. If one is not to please oneself in old age, when is one to please oneself? There is so little time left!" (67).

Her children think she is mad, or senile, except for Edith, who looks at her mother with new eyes: "It now dawned on Edith that her mother might have lived a full, private life, all these years, behind the shelter of her affectionate watchfulness. How much had she observed? noted? criticized? stored up?" (69). Only after the crisis of losing her husband is Lady Shane able (or willing) to live out her long repressed dreams, and only now does just one of her children regard her as a flesh-and-blood woman who had a rich inner life during all those years of gentility, service, and submission to family and culture.

But now the adventure of living alone gives Lady Shane a new consciousness and sensation of living, one that was "curious and interesting." On a train ride to Hampstead, she thinks about her life, her mind, "alert as ever, perhaps more alert, sharpened by the sense of imminent final interruption, spurred by the necessity of making the most of remaining time" (79). She is also aware of the frail inadequacies of her body, and how younger people, when they do notice these deficiencies, are slightly irritated. Yet now, alone, she does not feel old, but younger than she had in years, and "the proof of it was that she eagerly accepted this start of a new lap in life, even though it may be the last" (80).

A continent away from Eva, along with a lifetime of privilege, yet Lady Shane longs for the same: to make decisions, to live peacefully, *not* to be distracted by babies thrust on her lap. Brasher than Eva, she finds a voice that tells the truth: "I am going to become completely self-indulgent" (67). She fantasizes about her new life in her Hampstead cottage: no grandchildren ("too young"), no great-grandchildren ("that would be even worse"). She wants no one around her except "those who are nearer to their death than to their birth" (68).

What is the example of Lady Shane's life? She tells us that life at her age conceived as a remaining "lap" still has meaning and adventure if (health a given) one summons courage and determination, and puts to rest living a culturally scripted role of dependency and fear of the unknown.

THE ENDURING SPIRIT

Men have facilities for woodwork, work in metal and basket work. . . . The ladies have sewing classes, instruction in cooking and dancing classes.
—Anderson and Williams 1989, 14

Women and work: a persistent problem for women of all ages in a patriarchic culture that manages to infuse sexuality and power into the dailiness of women's labor—from the pink-collar ghettos to the glass ceilings of corporations to women's unpaid labor in homes. The work-related problems of women are difficult to face even when they have youth as a weapon: harassment, invisibility, overt and subtle discrimination. But aging has a special stain for women, especially those whose selves were defined in part by work outside homes. The marketplace screams to older women, "Old is ugly and unnatural in a society where power is male-defined, powerlessness disgraceful" (Rich in Macdonald 1983, 778). And, according to Copper (1986), there is another issue here:

The problem for old women is a problem of power. . . . the roles reserved and expected of women in old age—grandmothers, self-effacing volunteers to the projects and priorities designed by others, or caretakers of old men—are custom fit to our powerless status. (56)

Thus, old women's creative energies are deprecated in advance as they are kept out of the mainstream of productive life. (Healey 1986, 61) writes:

> We have put old women in nursing "homes" with absolutely no intellectual stimulation, isolated from human warmth and nurturing contact, and then condemned them for their senility. We have impoverished, disrespected, and disregarded old women, and then dismissed them as inconsequential and uninteresting. We have made old women invisible so that we do not have to confront our patriarchal myths about what makes life valuable or dying painful.

The literary accounts of the following women defy these patriarchic, ageist attempts to categorize and classify old women as invisible and powerless. They portray women who know that some of their options are gone or diminished, but who think of themselves as ongoing persons with much more to say and do.

Marilyn Zuckerman's poem, "After Sixty" (1987, 405), is a reflection on what she wants to find and how she wants to live "on the other side of sixty." Work, she wants—serious, passionate engagement with a project. She wants it all to be new, not a continuation of a lifelong project, but something that will appear after the knife has sliced into her future, piercing the culturally perceived flatness and finitude of life after sixty.

But why has she waited all her life for this kind of living? She writes:

> Doors have opened and shut
> The great distractions are over—
> passion . . . children . . . the long indenture of
> marriage.
> I fold them into a chest
> I will not take with me when I go.

Now, no longer distracted, she wants to "join forces with the strong old woman / to throw everything away and begin again," to invent herself and her new stories.

What will her work look like? She wants to fight the pornography of war with an activism that includes nonviolent resistance on many fronts, from defacing Trident submarine hulls to the walls of the Pentagon. And she wants to do it with women, to join them in other places on this planet,

> where women past the menopause
> put on tribal robes
> smoke pipes of wisdom
> —fly.

Poet Meridel LeSueur is doing away with the word "age." "Aging?" she writes. "You never hear of anything in nature aging, or a sunflower saying, 'Well, I'm growing old,' and leaning over and vomiting. You know, it *ripens*, it drops its seed and the cycle goes on. So I'm ripening" (1986, 9).

LeSueur finds the plight of postmenopausal women in contemporary North American culture pathetic, a position that is reflected in the content of her current work, and in the fact of her productivity well into her eighties. In her poem, "Rites of Ancient Ripening" (1982), her strong and mysterious connection to nature is distinct in the imagery she uses to connect herself to the cycles and fertility of the earth. She begins, "I am luminous with age" (261), a direct contradiction to predetermined standards of attractiveness, which is, of course, not old. She looks at herself and sees a lustrous and radiant woman whose "bones shine in fever / smoked with the fires of age" (261). She contains "the final juice" and lives "in the beloved bone / Speaking in the marrow / alive in green memory" (261). At 83, she is ripening in a world where family, work, social consciousness, and the earth are fused into the landscape, each refusing to be fenced off into discrete plots of her living. Her wish: "Release my seed and let me fall" (262) so that she may be lodged deep in the earth with her ancestors and children, and where her work can continue to nourish her and others as she grounds her corn daily.

When asked what she is working on now, she replies that one should not ask that of a person her age because the inevitable answer is that she is working on all that is unfinished, "getting in [her] crop before frost" (1986, 15). She refuses to think about literally finishing her work because "you don't finish a circle—but at least get turning in the ellipse before [you are] cut down by these dire things that come with age" (15). Now an old woman, an "old root," she is having the finest time of her life writing. Why? Because now

> The rites of ancient ripening
> Make my flesh plume
> And summer winds stir in my smoked bowl. (1982, 263)

"Crone: (1) a withered old woman esp. in humble circumstances (2) an old man useless or womanish from senility" (*Webster's Third New International Dictionary*, 1971). Disregarding, for now, the overt misogyny of the second definition, why would any woman *aspire* to become a crone?

In her essay, "The Space Crone," Ursula K. LeGuin finds the idea of old woman as crone instinctive. A crone, according to Le-Guin, is a spirit, a psyche, not a shell—an old woman who has become "pregnant with herself, at last," who gives birth to herself in her old age "with travail and alone" (1989, 5). No longer confusing her reproductive capacity with her self or her sexuality, a crone knows that childbearing (including the capacity) is not the only meaningful condition of women. But becoming a crone is a rite of passage many women evade, not because they want to—many are not even aware of its presence—but because they are seduced into the attempt to remain unchanged, young. It may be a gallant effort to remain unchanged, but LeGuin calls it "a stupid, self-sacrificial gallantry, better befitting a boy of twenty.... Let the athletes die young and laurel crowned. Let the soldiers earn the Purple Hearts. Let women die old, white-crowned, with human hearts" (5).

LeGuin creates a fiction about one of these white-crowned old women with a human heart. In this story she is faced with finding an exemplary person to send to the fourth planet of Altair. She knows exactly who she would look for and where she would find her, and it would not be a young man or woman in peak physical condition, in Washington or New York City for a powerful Kissinger-type bureaucrat. Instead she would find an accidental heroine, an over-sixty woman who works at the local Woolworth behind the costume jewelry counter. Never having sought the secret of eternal youth, this old woman looks her age. She is a crone. She has worked hard all of her life at small, unimportant jobs

> like cooking, cleaning, bringing up kids, selling little objects of
> adornment or pleasure to old people.... She never was edu-

cated to anything like her capacity, and that is a shameful waste and a crime against humanity, but so common a crime. . . . And anyhow she's not dumb. She has a stock of sense, wit, patience, and experiential shrewdness which the Altaireans might, or might not, perceive as wisdom. (6)

LeGuin guesses that it would be difficult to persuade the old woman to leave, or even to convince her that she was worthy of the trip. It would be hard to explain to her "that we want her to go because only a person who has experienced, accepted, and acted the entire human condition . . . can fairly represent humanity" (6). That is what a crone really is: withered, yes, but who is also the bearer of a human heart and mind that became so by living deeply and fully, who has never dodged or evaded her womanhood, and who is "facing the final birth/death a little more nearly and clearly every day" (6).

Returning to May Sarton, we find her this time at seventy, continuing to work at her lifelong craft of writing. She begins the task of writing a journal, *At Seventy*, that records her seventieth year, a life full of writing, gardening, friends, travel, solitude, and reflection. She tries to answer her own question, "What is it like to be seventy?", weaving partial responses throughout many entries. Her first musing: "I do not feel old at all, not as much as a survivor as a person still on her way. I suppose real old age begins when one looks backward rather than forward, but I look forward with joy to the years ahead and especially to the surprise that any day may bring" (1984, 10). Never avoiding the kind of reflection that uncovers accumulated grief, Sarton also describes middle of night wakefulness when things well up from the past—"the unsolved, the painful encounters, the mistakes, the reasons for shame or woe" (10).

Sarton repeats several times throughout the journal that she has always "looked forward" to being old, a statement often met by the not-old with suspicion or incredulity. Because of what North American culture usually associates with aging, most notably failing bodies and faculties, such an assertion is puzzling. But given the reflective life that writing has brought her, her answer to what was so good about being old makes sense: "I am more myself than I have ever been. There is less conflict. I am happier, more balanced, and . . . better able to use my powers" (10).

Sarton makes several absorbing observations comparing youth and old age that mark her belief in the gifts of both. One has to do with what she calls the genius of youth, which is "the curiosity, the intense interest in everything from a bird to a book to a dog," and the genius of old, which is "so much subtler and gentler, so much wiser" (76). She is working her way toward the latter, so that now, at seventy, she is able to live more completely in the moment; is less anxious about what is in the future; and is more removed from sources of pain, the loss of love, the struggle to accomplish/get finished, and the fear of death. Finally, she offers a comforting assurance that what gives a person joy need not have anything to do with age. For Sarton, these joys come from her garden, the light cast at different times of day, music, poetry, silence, birds—pleasures that may in fact deepen and enlarge over a lifetime.

BEYOND HAGS AND OLD MAIDS

The Body

The vagina is easily traumatized and is a not
infrequent cause of postmenopausal bleeding.
This may be slight but on occasion can be
quite marked from a tear due to splitting of the
vagina following infrequent coitus. . . . There is
a redistribution of fat with alteration in breast
contour. Postmenopausal breasts tend to be
pendulous, although they gradually diminish
in size.
                              —McEwan 1985, 155–56

The financial and emotional energy many twentieth-century women spend to slow down or reverse the aging of their bodies is extraordinary, miserable, and not surprising. "Having spent our lives estranged from our own bodies in the effort to meet that outer patriarchal standard of beauty," Healey writes, "it is small wonder that the prospect of growing old is frightening to women of all ages" (1986, 60). The relentless image of the unlined face and smooth, taut body begins to erode the spirit, confidence, and esteem of many women as soon as they are able to interpret the ubiquitous cultural codes that value youth and deprecate age, the double whammy in a culture that is both ageist and sexist. The following poems portray some older women's impressions as they look at their aging bodies with their own eyes, and as they project how others view them as well. Such impressions tell us how difficult it often is to match the "outward me with the me inside" (Healey, 58).

Randall Jarrell's poem, "Next Day" (1963), records an aging woman's awareness of her changing life and changing body. Grocery shopping, "moving from Cheer to Joy, from Joy to All," this woman feels the absence of eyes on her face, her body, her physical womanness. As the boy puts groceries in her car in the parking lot, her only wish now that she is old is that he *see* her, a "womanish" wish she calls it. By see, of course, she means look appreciatively. But he does not, nor does anyone else, not any more. She remembers how they used to:

> It bewilders me he doesn't see me.
> For so many years
> I was good enough to eat: the world looked at me
> And its mouth watered. How often they have
>   undressed me,
> The eyes of strangers! (3)

Now, looking in the rearview mirror, she meets a face that makes her fearful. The eyes, she hates; the smile, she hates. She hates "the plain, lined look / of gray discovery" that repeats to her " 'You're old.' That's all, I'm old" (4). She thinks back to her friend's funeral she attended the day before, how her friend's "cold made-up face" looked, and how young her friend had told her she appeared. For a moment, she has a respite from the fear and malaise of aging, but it quickly dissipates when she thinks about standing beside her own grave, "confused with [her] life, that is commonplace and / solitary" (5).

Her preoccupation with her face, with people looking at her appreciatively—even anonymous young boys in grocery stores—is tied to a conception of self defined by her family needing her less: "Today I miss / My lovely daughter / Away at school, my sons away at school, / My husband away at work" (4). Her changing face is indicative of these changes in her life; the fact that her "sure unvarying days," lived at home in the presence, shadows and ghosts of her family, will indeed change causes her fear. Without looking at her, the grocery store boy pats her dog, and now *she* is good. It appears to her that there is very little left since her "girlish" wish of a husband, house, and children has been fulfilled. Only now, her "womanish" desire is that someone, even a boy, would look at her.

One answer a woman may choose to deny the outward effect of aging involves cosmetic surgery. The answer is limited, of course, to the privileged, since most health care benefits do not include reimbursement for such nonessential procedures. Still, it is an option chosen by some women, and is symptomatic of the ageism deeply embedded in current North American culture.

Lisel Mueller's poem, "Face Lift" (1986b, 21), presents some arresting questions arising from a newly face-lifted woman. The first line sets in motion the startling question of how old someone really is if she has been altered to appear younger: "The woman who used to be my age." Spotting the changed woman in a grocery store, the onlooker begins silently posing questions about the woman's new face and what it means. Never talking directly to the face-lifted woman, she wonders what happened to the years that had been indelibly sculpted on her face: lines, bags, crinkles, crow's feet. Where were remnants of smiles, the looks of dread, the expressions of sadness and grief? Now, her face "has retracted sleepless nights, / denies any knowledge of pain," along with the dark eyes left by mourning someone she loved. Memories etched into her face are gone, and the onlooker wonders "how it feels to remember, / under the skin of a thirty-year-old, something that happened at forty."

She wonders how the woman's husband feels, if he is excited by "her new half-strangeness," or if he feels betrayed because she has "removed their years together." She cannot tell, because the woman's "unused face reveals nothing" here among the bell peppers and endive. No match now between her lived inner life and the face reflecting that life; what was important to this face-lifted woman was that her face match what the patriarchic, ageist culture prized. In this grocery store, perhaps the bagger of groceries now looks at her appreciatively, young man to older woman; likewise, the mirror now sends back a pleasing younger image that defies her lived years and experiences.

Lillian Morrison's "Body" (1987, 74) offers an affectionate accepting relationship between an old woman and her body. Using cat imagery this woman thinks of herself not as a cat, but living *with* "this big cat," an alter ego of sorts, a smooth, self-within-the-self. Referring to the cat as "it," she is, nonetheless, warmly familiar with and deeply committed to it: "Though it is / Aging now, I cannot abandon it / nor do I want to." She has accepted this changed state of her cat companion without too much difficulty, because what counts now are other ways of being in relationship. The cat is, for her,

> really pleasant to be with,
> familiar, faithful, complaining
> a little, continually going about
> its business, loving to lie down.

It is wonderfully interesting to note that the woman, the cat's companion, has not grown old, or at least her age is not referred to in the same way. The cat has aged, and the woman, patient cohabitator, is aware of the changes, and is a bit sad her cat cannot do what it once could. Yet she is gently, matter-of-factly accepting. Our selves/bodies are tangled yet sometimes seem distinct, weaving back and forth, one informing the other, edges blurred.

Lisel Mueller's poem "Fugitive" (1986a, 66) portrays a similar body/self split, not to advance a dualism that wrests flesh from spirit, but as a means to think about mixed self images, wrought from disparate, confusing cultural cues. The woman begins, "My life is running away with me / the two of us are in cahoots," but tells the reader wryly that she is holding still while "it"—her fleshy self—paints dark circles under her eyes, streaks her hair with gray, and pads her body with layers under her clothes. The woman does not lament these changes, although she appears to be a passive recipient, but not really victim, of these changes. She is so changed that every time she passes a mirror, her self-*in*-the-body, the "I" of the poem, is reassured by the mirror that she will be unrecognized. This self embodied in the masqueraded flesh is "learning to travel light" with her "I" baggage that has been "swallowed by memory," now weighing almost nothing in an essential, vaporous state more authentic than any flesh. No one knows how valuable her "I" is, or even that it is there embedded in her changing flesh. In fact, when "they"—the friends, lovers, and others—come looking for her but see only the changed flesh, they turn away, because she "doesn't match their description." When she closes the door on this search party, she catches a glimpse of that other, her fleshy life, who winks at her from the corner, and "wipes off [her] fingerprints."

The woman seems relieved at this very real masquerade. Helpless, perhaps unwilling to try to stop, reverse, or slow down the aging of her body, this woman is an accomplice—"in cahoots"—with nature regarding her flesh, insofar as she does not fight the aging. Rather, she recognizes her "I" as her most valuable, most vital self that no one can take from her. She makes no claim, however, that her "I" is a discrete entity uninformed by her outer self. Her implicit lament has more to do with others who equate her outer aging body with her inner self, and in patriarchic, ageist cultural environs, that only means trouble.

Yet sometimes an aging woman is stunned by the mismatch between her outer body and her inner sense of being. Sylvia Plath's poem "Mirror" (1981, 173–74), written in a mirror's voice describing a woman's complex, often angry relationship with her face, revisits the "mirror, mirror on the wall" phenomenon of childhood. Looking for validation, the woman bends over the mirror—"a lake"—to search its "reaches for what she really is." Disbelieving, she tries to hide what the mirror tells her, and she "turns to those liars, the candles or the moon." But the mirror does not lie, and reflects her image faithfully to be met with "tears and an agitation of hands." Still, the mirror is important to her, even though it reports

In me she has drowned a young girl, and in me an old woman
Rises toward her day after day, like a terrible fish.

Unlike Morrison's big, warm, aging cat, Plath's image of an aging woman as a "terrible" fish evokes a dread and self-loathing in the image reflected in the mirror. And unlike Morrison's aging woman whose identity is pleasantly affirmed even with her cat-body able to do less and less, Plath's aging woman has never learned to construct her identity, to validate herself, to like herself away from the mirror or in the reflection of herself in others' eyes, all increasingly difficult as a woman accumulates years in a sexist, ageist culture.

Last, the solitary women washing dishes in Sharon Mooney's poem "Is Every Kitchen Sink Under a Window?" is, like Mueller's and Morrison's narrators, amiably surrendering to her changing, aging body (1986, 108–9). Seeing her reflection in the mirror as she gropes for knives and scrapes food off plates, she muses:

i am surprised i like
my image
i look my age

Readers may wonder about the possible missing word between the second and third lines: Is she surprised that she likes her image *because* she looks her age? Or is she surprised she likes her image at all? That is, did she not like her image at one time, and now she does? Is the "i look my age" merely the next thought, and not a source of surprise?

Moments later, she looks again at the reflection in the window, and, pulling her skin back up against her hairline, sees and remembers what she looked like before "no lines not worn." We do not know what she thought looking at that erased face, but we know the image must not have caused great nostalgia or envy of her younger life or face because she

> let[s] go
> my flesh falls back
> i come home to my time
> my place
> i am my age.

"I look my age" and "i am my age" reveal a view of self that this woman has managed to achieve as she transcends, ignores, even scorns the predictable, pervasive scriptures of a youth-dominated culture. She does not tell us how she has escaped, but only that it can be done.

Sexuality

For women the availability of a sexually capable and societally sanctioned sexual partner appears to be the most important factor. Among men, marital status appears to be almost totally irrelevant to continued sexual activity.
                    —*Pfeiffer 1979, 569*

Sexuality is a delicate subject. Older women are embarrassed by talking about it.
                    —*Barber 1988, 236*

What happens to a woman's sexual expression as she ages, when she becomes "old"? Because of the intricate ties in this culture between desirability, physical attractiveness, youth, and sexu-

Käthe Kollwitz (German, 1867-1945). *Self-Portrait*, 1921. Etching on paper, 8½×10½ in. The National Museum of Women in the Arts.

ality, views on sexual expression in the old (from the perspectives of the not-old) range from humorous to pathetic, that is, if the old are perceived as sexual beings in the first place. The stories and poems below spurn those perceptions.

Gabriel Garcia Marquez's *Love in the Time of Cholera* (1988) chronicles the half century of love entwining three people: Florentino, a poet and businessman who has remained unmarried and has been in love with Fermina, who has had a long, sturdy, reasonably satisfying marriage to Juvenal, a prominent physician and one of the most illustrious men of his time. After fifty years, nine months, and four days of unrequited love, Florentino declares his love once again to Fermina, now a widow. They become lovers, finally, on a boat cruising up a river without cargo or passengers with a phony yellow plague flag flying to avoid every port and all human contact. Different now in their bodies and the expectations they have for each other, they do not feel like newlyweds in their new physical intimacy. Rather,

> it was as if they had leapt over the arduous calvary of conjugal life and gone straight to the heart of love. They were together in silence like an old married couple wary of life, beyond the pitfalls of passion, beyond the brutal mockery of hope and the phantoms of disillusion: beyond love. For they had lived together long enough to know that love was always love, anytime and anyplace, but it was more solid the closer it came to death. (345)

Still, in addition to the connection that seemed to transcend the physical, there was sensuousness. They spent "unimaginable hours holding hands in the armchairs by the railing, they exchanged unhurried kisses, they enjoyed the rapture of caresses without the pitfalls of impatience" (338). And she "accepted with pleasure" when Florentino "dared to explore her withered neck with his fingertips, her bosom armored in metal stays, her hips with their decaying bones, her thighs with their aging veins" (338). All this they did without guilt or shame, in spite of her shocked middle-aged children at home who believed that "there was an age at which love began to be indecent" (327). In a bitter argument with her brother over Florentino's presence in their mother's home, Fermina's daughter angrily insisted that "love is ridiculous at our age . . . but at theirs it is revolting" (323). Happily, for Fermina and Florentino, Fermina did not back away: "They can all go to hell. . . . If we widows have any advantage, it is that there is no one left to give us orders" (324).

Marcia Woodruff's poem "Love at Fifty" (1987) holds similar descriptions of women's aging sexual bodies. These lovers, who came together "shy as virgins," do not possess beauty or innocence. Rather, they bring to each other well lived-in bodies. One lover to the other:

> Our eyes are sadder and wiser
> as I finger the scar on your shoulder
> where the pin went in,
> and you touch the silver marks on my belly,
> loose from childbearing. (93)

Once more, the image of mirror, this time used to describe how, twenty years previously, they would have "turned one another into mirrors / so we could make love to ourselves." Now, clothed in "simple flesh" with "complicated histories" written on each, the two give each other themselves, in their bodies, which are "gifts / at the touch of [their] hands."

Adrienne Rich's numbered series, "Twenty-One Love Poems" (1978a), includes several illuminating references to love between two women who are "not young." Like Fermina and Florentino, their experience of love is physically passionate. At one point during the day, one of the women in the poem arrives home, her "body still both light and heavy with you" (26); another moment finds her remembering "your touch on me, firm, protective, searching / me out" (32). But the tender vitality of their relationship is the result, at least in part, of having experienced a life of "pure invention [since] / the maps they gave us were out of date" (31):

> Since we're not young, weeks have to do time
> for years of missing each other. Yet only this odd warp
> in time tells me we're not young.
> Did I ever walk the morning streets at twenty,
> my limbs streaming with a purer joy?
> . . . .
> I touch you knowing we weren't born tomorrow,
> and somehow, each of us will help the other live,
> and somehow, each of us must help the other die. (26)

In another line, the woman describes the "generous, delicate mouth" of her lover as a place "where grief and laughter sleep together." This "place" becomes a portrait of love and connection found later in life with its bittersweet and quiet intensity, where sadness for time lost yet revelry for the riches of passion and tenderness live together.

Michael Blumenthal's poem, "The Pleasures of Old Age" (1987), presents a different view of romantic love in old age. Instead of focusing on the wisdom and experience one brings to such a relationship, Lisette thinks only of the flesh. In fact, when she turned ninety-nine, "all she could think of was men," and not only for companionship. Instead, she would dream of them,

> how they would enter her room during the night
> from the vast mixer of the mind, wild
> with desire, drunk with a desperate love

for only her. . . .
she could dream them back in her arms,
those beautiful men, and when morning came,
rise from her immaculate bed, pink
with the glow of the newly deflowered. (101)

It appears that Lisette might mock us for romanticizing intimacy in
later years as something more authentic, more *real* than what we
find, or think we find, in the young. No matter what the age, physical intimacy may be a matter of seizing and savoring moments
without thought of where that relationship might lead. Here Lisette
makes us wonder why the thought of casual sex is more difficult to
conceive in the old but not in the more daring young; for Lisette it
is perfectly natural. One is reminded of the voice in Muriel Rukeyser's poem, "Rondel," which exalts her age and sexuality, and while
younger than Lisette, explains how things are "different":

What happens to song and sex
Now that I am fifty six?
They dance, but differently,
Death and distance in the mix. (1978, 497)

Perhaps with death and distance in sight, Lisette and others like her
dance to the body's moment, not waiting for other elusive
connections.

Finally, Alice Walker's poem, "Medicine," is a sadly sweet reminder that sexuality is also spirit, touch, and presence. Walker's
old woman, "Grandma," sleeps with her sick husband, ostensibly so
she can get him medicine in the middle of the night to stop the pain.
But the poem tells more than this seemingly straightforward gesture
of care: when awakened in the morning, Grandma cradled in his
"withered arms," what the observer comes to realize is that

Grandma sleeps with
my sick
grand-

pa so she
can get him
during the night
medicine
to stop

                    the pain
                         In
                    the morning
                     clumsily
                         I
                      wake
                       them

          Her eyes
          look at me
          from under-
                         neath
          his withered
          arm

                 The
               medicine
                is all
                   in
              her long
                  un-
                    braided hair.
                   (1991, 133–34)

---

*In nearly every species in which sex-specific
longevity variations have been studied in de-
tail, the female outlives the male. . . . This difference in life span has been attributed to the
more protected life of the woman. It has been
said, for example, that unlike the man, who
has to work under stress in highly competitive
civilizations, the modern woman has been released from the burden of housekeeping duties
by an increasing variety of mechanical devices.*
                              —Jarvik 1979, 89

   Here more than in any other section of this text, we had difficulty selecting literature for discussion. This is not because of a
scarcity of literature on the subject of women and aging; the choices
were extraordinarily expansive and rich. The knotty issue was "to
create new social symbols and transform misinformation that de-
bilitates all women who grow old" (Alexander et al. 1986, 6), even as

we acknowledge the continuing invisibility of old women who are not healthy or vibrant. Because our attempt has never focused on some kind of generalizability, we decided to select literature that assumed health, and to take this examination of women and aging into largely unexplored territory. Thus, the categories we used—"O blessed solitude," "The enduring spirit," and "Beyond hags and old maids"—assume relatively healthy and mobile bodies. Of course there are sick, lonely old women who do not savor solitude, who cannot continue doing meaningful work, and who are celibate by choice or chance. We did not consciously (or unconsciously) gloss over these women, but chose to limit our examination because of the insidious ageism of North American culture that does quite a handy job of portraying old women exclusively from those categories.

What we recorded here represents an attempt to disentangle the skein of an ageist and sexist culture, each selection an often overlooked or hidden strand in that skein. Most of these are women who, beginning that last lap, want to go the distance, and are aware of the distance.

Anatole Broyard, referring to the British psychoanalyst D. W. Winnicott's unfinished autobiography, quotes the fifth paragraph: "Let me see. What was happening when I died? My prayer had been answered. I was alive when I died. That was all I had asked and I had got it" (1991, 30).

If there is any predictability, most of the women portrayed here will be alive when they die, too.

Coda

Writing this book has been, for both of us, an experience full of conflicting and unpredictable encounters with ourselves. Some were gently connective, much like Toi Derricotte's description of birth, when she feels something pulling, a "soft call . . . wide and deep and wonderful" (33). As women who had experienced birth, albeit under conditions worlds apart from Derricotte's narrator, we *knew*, and reveled in the words Derricotte crafted to push us back into deep memory, keeping the event alive, supple, available.

Then we paused, and reconsidered: not all births ring with the words "joy, joy." Lucille Clifton tells us about that. And Kelly Cherry reminds us both about the hopelessness, profound sadness, and sometimes anger of many women who live through the cold, daily frustrations of infertility.

We were hopeful as we read some narrative voices telling us what they found beyond the watershed of women's reproductive selves in their old age: LeSueur's and Sarton's intellectual vigor, Zuckerman's political activism, LeGuin's crone wisdom. Yet we were frightened by the graphic ravages of illness. Closer now to menopause than puberty, we see disease lurking in more places. We read of the pain of breast cancer that cannot be named, but which was expressed with such bittersweet pathos in the fictions we read, causing us to touch and look at ourselves again, wondering, fearful, feeling whatever pain we could for this women's plague that will not go away.

Throughout this confrontation with our selves, we often looked up from our reading and out on the culture that begins the patriarchic kneading and molding of girls literally at birth with the following dicta: first, last, and always stay thin and firm; ward off/ hide external evidence of aging; remember that physical attractiveness is more important than other intangibles when it comes to sexuality and desirability; recognize that reproductive capacities are critical to the maintenance of female identity.

And we are sad and outraged. In our separate and various lives we endlessly talk, argue, admonish; we try the seduction of reason, the power of narrative, the singular voice of our experience. We teach, serve on committees, write papers and letters, give money, protest. And just when we think we are beginning to recognize the multiple meanings of women's oppression, a moment, a word, an event, a glance stops us in our tracks, and we witness again thoughtless or thought out crimes against the bodies and spirits of women, some that occur right before us, some that are brought to us in stories. Some of these stories are found in the preceding pages.

How can and do stories take us deep into ourselves, and then beyond ourselves? Joe David Bellamy (1992) writes about the power of the arts and their ability to transform, inspire, and transcend:

> Real art is about imagination, empathy, emotion, and aesthetic and poetic truth, and it teaches us how to be more skillful in these domains. Real art is about getting through life and finding meaning in it and trying to understand and remember it. We need the literary artist because he or she . . . pricks our consciences. . . . As Lady Murasaki says in her *Tale of Genji* when she's asked by the Prince why she writes, "So there will be never a time when people don't know these things happened." Literature is our . . . treasury of language and style and our best reckoning about human life, as it is lived in this time and place. (669)

This is our hope for readers as they weave together these stories, their lives, and other women's lives. As the power of the imagination is unleashed—a power casting new lights and lifting shadows on both our private lives and those collective gendered experiences involving our women's bodies and health—we may be moved to form those alliances necessary for improving the lives of all women.

"Our experience," Martha Nussbaum reminds us, "is too confined and too parochial. Literature extends it, making us reflect and feel about what might be too distant for feeling" (1990, 47). Further, literature cultivates our sympathies to an expansive realm of problems and worries, and develops aversions to "certain denials of humanity" as well (47).

   While the stories here (and probably the readers who pick up this book) represent only a few snapshots of the women of this world, their images need to be seen, treated tenderly and thoughtfully, and then placed beside those of other women in a localized fashion, interlaced with commonalities, differences, and even conflicts. The authors, the text and its readers: each and together a part, we desire, of a multilayered feminist solidarity.

Bibliography

Alexander, J., Berrow, D., Domitrovich, L., Donnelly, M., McLean, C. (eds.). 1986. *Women and aging: An anthology by women.* Corvallis, Oreg.: Calyx Books.

Alvarez, J. 1991. *How the garcia girls lost their accents.* New York: Workman Publishing Co.

Anderson, F., and Williams, B. 1989. *Practical management of the elderly,* 5th ed. Oxford: Blackwell Scientific Publications.

Apter, T. 1990. *Altered loves: Mothers and daughters during adolescence.* New York: St. Martin's Press.

Atwood, M. 1986. *The handmaid's tale.* Boston: Houghton Mifflin.

————. 1977. Giving birth. In *Dancing girls and other stories* (225–40). New York: Simon and Schuster.

Bambara, T. C. 1977. A girl's story. In *The sea birds are still alive* (152–65). New York: Random House.

Barber, H. R. K. 1988. *Perimenopausal and geriatric gynecology.* New York: Macmillan.

Barkin, R. M., and Rosen, P. 1990. *Emergency pediatrics: A guide to ambulatory care.* St. Louis: C. V. Mosby.

Barrington, J. ed. 1988. *An intimate wilderness: Lesbian writers on sexuality.* Portland, Oreg.: Eighth Mountain Press.

Bass, E. 1975. First menstruation. In *On separateness and merging* (50). Brookline, Mass.: Autumn Press.

Bellamy, J. D. 1992. On pens and swords. *The Nation* (668–72). November 30.

Blumenthal, M. 1987. The pleasures of old age. In *Against romance* (101). New York: Viking.

Bogdan, D. 1990. Censorship, identification, and the poetics of need. In A. Lunsford, H. Moglen, and J. Slevin (eds.), *The right to literacy* (128–47). New York: Modern Language Association.

Braunwald, E. et al., eds. 1987. *Harrison's principles of internal medicine,* 11th ed. (1822–24). New York: McGraw-Hill.

Brooks, G. 1963. The mother. In *Selected poems* (4). New York: Harper and Row.

Brownmiller, S. 1975. *Against our will.* New York: Bantam.

Broyard, A. 1992. *Intoxicated by my illness: And other writings on life and death.* New York: Clarkson Potter Publishers.

Brunner, L. S., and Suddarth, D. S. 1992. *Textbook of medical-surgical nursing* (1291–1322). Philadelphia: Lippincott.

Burgess, A. W., and Holmstrom, L. L. 1978. Accessory to sex: Pressure, sex and secrecy. In A. Wolbert, A. N. Groth, L. L. Holmstrom, and S. Sgroi (eds.), *Sexual assault of children and adolescents* (85–98). Lexington, Mass.: Lexington Books.

Chasin, H. 1968. The recovery room: Lying in. In *Coming close and other poems* (19). New Haven: Yale University Press.

Cherry, K. 1990. What I don't tell people. In J. Mukand (ed.), *Vital lines: Contemporary fiction about medicine* (200–214). New York: St. Martin's Press.

Cixous, H. 1991. Coming to writing. In D. Jenson (ed.), *Coming to writing and other essays,* trans. S. Cornell, D. Jenson, A. Liddle, S. Sellers (1–58). Cambridge: Harvard University Press.

———. 1990. Castration or decapitation? In R. Ferguson, M. Gever, T. T. Minh-ha, and C. West (eds.), *Out there: Marginalization and contemporary cultures* (345–56). Cambridge: MIT Press.

———. 1976. The laugh of the medusa. Trans. K. Cohen and P. Cohen. *Signs: Journal of Women in Culture and Society* 1(4):875–93.

Clarke-Pearson, D., and Dawood, M. Y. 1990. *Green's gynecology: Essentials of clinical practice.* Boston: Little, Brown.

Clifton, L. 1991a. to my last period. In *Quilting: Poems 1987–1990 (59).* Brockport, N.Y.: BOA Limited Editions.

———. 1991b. poem to my uterus. In *Quilting: Poems 1987–1990* (58). Brockport, N.Y.: BOA Limited Editions.

———. 1991c. eyes. In *Quilting: Poems 1987–1990* (21–23). Brockport, N.Y.: BOA Limited Editions.

———. 1987a. she understands me. In *Good woman: Poems and a memoir 1969–1980* (137). Brockport, N.Y.: BOA Limited Editions.

———. 1987b. the lost baby poem. In *Good woman: Poems and a memoir 1969–1980* (60–61). Brockport, N.Y.: BOA Limited Editions.

Cooper, B. 1986. Voices: On becoming an old woman. In J. Alexander et al. (eds.), *Women and aging: An anthology by women* (47–57). Corvallis, Oreg.: Calyx, Inc.

Derricotte, T. 1983. *Natural childbirth.* Freedom, Calif: Crossing Press.

Didion, J. 1970. *Play it as it lays.* New York: Farrar, Straus and Giroux.

Dilts, P. V., Green, J. W., and Roddick, J. W. 1970. *Core studies in obstretrics and gynecology,* 2nd ed. Baltimore: Williams and Wilkins.

Downing, C. 1991. Quoted in D. Taylor and A. C. Sumrall (eds.), *Women of the 14th moon* (np). Freedom, Calif.: Crossing Press.

Drabble, M. 1965. *The millstone.* London: Weidenfeld and Nicholson.

Dunker, P. 1992. Sisters and strangers: An introduction to contemporary feminist fiction. Oxford UK: Blackwell Publishers.

Dworkin, P. H. 1987. *Pediatrics.* New York: John Wiley and Sons.

Emans, S. J. H., and Goldstein, D. P. 1990. *Pediatric and adolescent gynecology,* 3rd ed. Boston: Little, Brown.

Enelow, A., and Devine, M. 1982. Individual counseling and social support in the treatment of cancer patients. In S. Carter, E. Glatstein, R. Livingston (eds.), *Principles of cancer treatment* (268–72). New York: McGraw-Hill.

Epps, J. C. 1990. On cancer and conjuring. In E. C. White (ed.), *The black women's health book* (38–43). Seattle: Seal Press.

Fields, D. H. 1990. Conduct of normal labor. In H. R. Barber, D. H. Fields, and S. A. Kaufman (eds.), *Quick reference to OB-GYN procedures* (75–77). Philadelphia: Lippincott.

Firestone, S. 1970. *The dialectic of sex.* New York: Bantam Books.

Frank, D., and Brackley, M. 1989. The health experience of single women who have children through artificial donor insemination. *Clinical Nurse Specialist* 3(3):156–60.

Fraser, N., and Nicholson, L. 1990. Social criticism without philosophy: An encounter between feminism and postmodernism. In L. Nicholson (ed.) *Feminism/postmodernism* (133–56). New York: Routledge.

Gale, Z. (1988). Jonesie. In L. Lifshitz (ed.), *Her soul beneath the bone* (49). Urbana: University of Illinois Press.

Garcia Marquez, G. 1988. *Love in the time of cholera.* New York: Knopf.

Gath, D., and Rose, N. 1985. Psychological problems and gynaecological surgery. In R. G. Priest (ed.), *Psychological disorders in obstetrics and gynaecology* (31–48). London: Butterworths.

Goedicke, P. 1988. One more time. In L. Lifshitz (ed.), *Her soul beneath the bone* (2). Urbana: University of Illinois Press.

Griffith-Kenney, J. 1986. *Contemporary women's health: A nursing advocacy approach.* Menlo Park, Calif.: Addison-Wesley.

Harding, S. 1988. The instability of the analytical categories of feminist theory. In S. Harding and J. O'Barr (eds.), *Sex and scientific inquiry* (283–302). Chicago: University of Chicago Press.

Harris, J. 1988. The lump the swelling the possibility of cancer: Notes from the oncology clinic. In L. Lifshitz (ed.), *Her soul beneath the bone* (24–29). Urbana: University of Illinois Press.

Harrison, J. 1991. *Just before dark.* Boston: Houghton Mifflin/Seymour Lawrence.

Healey, S. 1986. Growing to be an old woman: Aging and ageism. In J. Alexander et al. (eds.), *Women and aging: An anthology by women* (58–62). Corvallis, Oreg.: Calyx Books.

Henderson-Holmes, S. 1990. Snapshots of Grace. In T. McMillan (ed.), *Breaking ice: An anthology of contemporary African-American fiction* (331–42). New York: Penguin Books.

Hoffert, S. 1989. *Private matters.* Springfield: Univesity of Illinois Press.

hooks, b. 1991. *Yearning: Race, gender, and cultural politics. Boston: South End Press.*

Humphrey, M. 1991. Virgin births (letter). *The Lancet* 337 (8744): 798.

Iser, W. 1978. *The act of reading: A theory of aesthetic response.* Baltimore: Johns Hopkins University Press.

Jack, D. 1991. Silencing the self. *Women and depression* (161–83). Boston: Harvard University Press.

Jakobsen, S., Beckmann, J., Beckmann, M., and Brunner, S. 1987. Mammography: Attitudes and reactions. In S. Brunner and B. Langfelt (eds.), *Recent results in cancer research: Breast cancer* (73–77). Berlin: Springer-Verlag.

Jarrell, R. 1963. Next day. In *The lost world* (3–4). New York: Macmillan.

Jarvik, L. F. 1979. Genetic aspects of aging. In I. Rossman (ed.), *Clinical geriatrics*, 2nd ed. (86–109). Philadelphia: Lippincott.

Kandinsky, C. 1991. As a woman grows older. In D. Taylor and A. C. Sumrall (eds), *Women of the 14th moon* (30). Freedom, Calif.: Crossing Press.

Kaye/Kantrowitz, M. 1988. eyes. In J. Barrington (ed.), *An intimate wilderness: Lesbian writers on sexuality* (131–32). Portland, Oreg.: Eighth Mountain Press.

Kelley, W. N., ed. 1989. *Textbook of internal medicine.* Philadelphia: Lippincott.

Kirby, V. 1991. Corporeal habits: Addressing essentialism differently. *Hypatia* 6(3):4–24.

Kolodny, A. 1985. Dancing through the minefield: Some observations on the theory, practice, and politics of a feminist literary criticism. In E. Showalter (ed.), *The new French feminisms: Essays on women, literature, and theory* (144–67). New York: Pantheon Books.

Koonin, L. M., Atrash, H. K., Smith, J. C., and Ramich, M. 1990. *Morbidity and mortality weekly report.* U.S. Department of Health and Human Services, Public Health Service, Centers for Disease Control (23).

Koplow, G. 1991. Eggs. In D. Taylor and A. C. Sumrall (eds.), *Women of the 14th moon* (145–46). Freedom, Calif.: Crossing Press.

Kushner, R. 1988. Foreword to L. Lifshitz (ed.), *Her soul beneath the bone* (xiii–xvi). Urbana: University of Illinois Press.

Laros, R. K. 1991. Physiology of normal pregnancy. In J. R. Willson and E. R. Carrington (eds.), *Obstetrics and gynecology* (232–46). St. Louis: Mosby Year Book.

Lather, P. 1992. Postmodernism and the human sciences. In S. Kvale (ed.), *Psychology and postmodernism* (88–109). London: Sage.

——. 1991. *Getting smart: Feminist research and pedagogy with/in the postmodern.* New York: Routledge.

——. 1986. Issues of validity in openly ideological research. *Interchange* 17(4): 63–84.

Lawrence, K. R. 1986. *Maud Gone.* New York: Atheneum Press.

Leach, G. 1970. *The biocrats.* New York: McGraw Hill.

Leavitt, J. 1986. *Brought to bed.* New York: Oxford University Press.

LeGuin, U. K. 1989. The space crone. In *Dancing at the edge of the world.* New York: Grove Press.

Lerner, G. 1986. *The creation of patriarchy.* New York: Oxford University Press.

LeSueur, M. 1986. Remarks from 1983 poetry reading. In J. Alexander et al. (eds.), *Women and aging: An anthology by women* (9–19). Corvallis, Oreg.: Calyx Books.

———. 1982. Rites of ancient ripening. In *Ripening* (261–64). Old Westbury, N.Y.: Feminist Press.

Levertov, D. 1975. A woman alone. In *Life in the forest* (16–17). New York: A New Directions Book.

Lifshitz, L. H. ed. 1988. *Her soul beneath the bone.* Urbana: University of Illinois Press.

Lorde, A. 1980. *The cancer journals.* San Francisco: Aunt Lute/Spinsters Ink.

Macdonald, B. (with Cynthia Rich). 1983. *Look me in the eye: Old women, aging, and ageism.* San Francisco: Spinsters Ink.

MacKinnon, C. 1982. Feminism, marxism, method, and the state: An agenda for theory. *Signs: Journal of Women in Culture and Society* 7(3):515–44.

Madaras, L. 1991. The changes of puberty. In A. Pedersen and P. O'Mara (eds.), *Teens: A fresh look* (53–71). Santa Fe, N. Mex.: John Muir Publications.

Martin, W. 1990. *We are the stories we tell.* New York: Pantheon.

Mason, B. A. 1988. *Spence + lila.* New York: Harper & Row.

McCann, J. 1991. Forty-five. In D. Taylor and A. C. Sumrall (eds.), *Women of the 14th moon* (144). Freedom, Calif.: Crossing Press.

McEwan, H. P. 1985. Management of the menopause. In M. C. Macnaughton (ed.), *Medical gynaecology* (154–74). Oxford: Blackwell Scientific Publications.

McPherson, S. 1970. Pregnancy. In *Elegies for the hot season* (55–56). Bloomington: Indiana University Press.

Metzger, D. (1988). I am no longer afraid. In L. Lifshitz (ed.), *Her soul beneath the bone* (71). Urbana: University of Illinois Press.

Middleton, K. L. (1988). Mastectomy. In L. Lifshitz (ed.), *Her soul beneath the bone* (39). Urbana: University of Illinois Press.

Miller, N. K. 1991. *Getting personal: Feminist occasions and other autobiographical acts.* New York: Routledge.

Minh-ha, T. T. 1989. *Woman native other.* Bloomington: Indiana University Press.

Mitford, J. 1992. *The American way of birth.* New York: Dutton.

Mooney, S. 1986. Is every kitchen sink under a window? In J. Alexander et al. (eds.), *Women and aging: An anthology by women* (108–9). Corvallis, Oreg.: Calyx Books.

Morantz-Sanchez, R. 1985. *Science and sympathy.* New York: Oxford University Press.

Morrison, L. 1987. Body. In S. Martz (ed.), *When I am an old woman I shall wear purple* (74). Watsonville, Calif.: Papier-Mache Press.

Morrison, T. 1970. *The bluest eye.* New York: Washington Square Press.

Mueller, L. 1986a. Fugitive. In *Second language* (66). Baton Rouge: Louisiana State University Press.

———. 1986b. Face-lift. In *Second language* (21). Baton Rouge: Louisiana State University Press.

———. 1980. Why we tell stories. In *The need to hold still (62–63).* Baton Rouge: Louisiana State University Press.

Mukand, J. (ed.) 1990. *Vital lines: Contemporary fiction about medicine.* New York: St. Martin's Press.

Nadelson, C. 1978. Normal and special aspects of pregnancy: A psychological approach. In *The woman patient: Medical and psychological interfaces* (73–86). New York: Plenum Press.

Naylor, G. 1982. *The women of brewster place: A novel in seven stories.* New York: Viking Penguin.

Nussbaum, M. C. 1990. Introduction: Form and content, philosophy and literature. In *Love's knowledge: Essays on philosophy and literature* (3-53). New York: Oxford University Press.

Oates, J. C. 1982. Baby. In *Invisible woman* (11). Ontario: Ontario Review Press.

Olds, S. 1987. The girl. In *The gold cell* (14–15). New York: Alfred A. Knopf.

————. 1983. 35/10. In *The dead and the living* (75). New York: Alfred A. Knopf.

Olsen, T. [1956] 1976. *Tell me a riddle.* New York: Dell.

Pastan, L. 1985. Routine mammogram. In *A fraction of darkness* (46–47). New York: W. W. Norton.

————. 1982. Notes from the delivery room. In *PM/AM* (26). New York: W. W. Norton.

Patrick, M. 1986. Characteristics of the aged population. In D. Carnevali and M. Patrick (eds.), *Nursing management for the elderly,* 2nd ed. (53–64). Philadelphia: Lippencott.

Pfeiffer, E. 1979. Sexuality and aging. In I. Rossman (ed.), *Clinical geriatrics,* 2nd ed. (568–75). Philadelphia: Lippincott.

Piercy, M. 1988. Something to look forward to. In *Available light* (26–27). New York: Alfred A. Knopf.

Plath, S. [1961] 1981. Mirror. In *The collected poems* (173–74). New York: Harper & Row.

Ponce, M. H. 1987. La doctora barr. In E. Vigil (ed.), *Woman of her word: Hispanic women write* (113–15). Houston: Arte Publico Press.

Quinby, L. 1992. *Freedom, Foucault, and the subject of America.* Boston: Northeastern University Press.

Reitz, R. 1991. Foreword to D. Taylor and A. C. Sumrall (eds.), *Women of the 14th moon: Writings on menopause* (iii–vi). Freedom, Calif.: Crossing Press.

Rich, A. 1978a. Twenty-one love poems. In *The dream of a common language: Poems 1974–1977* (26, 31–32). New York: W. W. Norton.

————. 1978b. A woman dead in her forties. In *The dream of a common language* (53–58). New York: W. W. Norton.

————. 1976. Of woman born: Motherhood as experience and institution. New York: W. W. Norton.

Riley, T. 1991. Commercial messages. In D. Taylor and A. C. Sumrall (eds.), *Women of the 14th moon* (140–43). Freedom, Calif.: Crossing Press.

Rosenblum, B. 1991. Cancer in two voices: Living in an unstable body. In J. Barrington (ed.), *An intimate wilderness: Lesbian writers on sexuality* (133–38). Portland, Oreg.: Eighth Mountain Press.

Rukeyser, M. 1978. Rondel. In *The collected poems of Muriel Rukeyser.* New York: McGraw-Hill.

Sackville-West, V. [1931] 1984. *All passion spent*. Garden City, N.Y.: Dial Press.

Sarton, M. 1984. *At seventy*. New York: W. W. Norton.

———. 1973. *Journal of a solitude*. New York: W. W. Norton.

Schain, W. 1978. Guidelines for psychological management of breast cancer: A stage-related approach. In H. S. Gallager, H. P. Leis, Jr., R. K. Snyderman, and J. A. Urban (eds.), *The breast* (465–75). St. Louis: C. V. Mosby.

Scherer, J. 1991. Disorders of the female reproductive system and related structures. In J. Scherer (ed.), *Introductory medical-surgical nursing*, 5th ed. (669–706). Philadelphia: Lippincott.

Schodek, K. (1988). Mastectomy. In L. Lifshitz (ed.), *Her soul beneath the bone* (40). Urbana: University of Illinois Press.

Schwartz, L. S. 1987. So you're going to have a new body! In *The melting poet (and other subversive stories)* (42-58). New York: Harper & Row.

Schweickart, P. 1986. Toward a feminist theory of reading. In E. Flynn and P. Schweickart (eds.), *Gender and reading: Essays on readers, texts, and contexts* (31–62). Baltimore: Johns Hopkins University Press.

Scott, J. 1988. Deconstructing equality-versus-difference: Or, the uses of poststructuralist theory for feminism. *Feminist Studies* 14(1):33–50.

Seltzer, J. 1991. No more x's on my calendar, no more PMS. In D. Taylor and A. C. Sumrall (eds.), *Women of the 14th moon* (25). Freedom, Calif.: Crossing Press.

Sexton, A. 1960. Unknown girl in the maternity ward. In *To bedlam and part way back* (34–35). New York: Houghton Mifflin.

Sherwin, S. 1992. No longer patient: Feminist ethics and health care. Philadelphia: Temple University Press.

Silko, L. M. 1977. *Ceremony*. New York: Penguin.

Skramstad, S. 1992. *The singing teacher*. Chapel Hill, N.C.: Algonquin Books of Chapel Hill.

Sloane, E. 1985. *Biology of women*. New York: John Wiley and Sons.

Smiley, J. 1991. *A thousand acres*. New York: Alfred A. Knopf.

Snyderman, A. E., and Snyderman, R. K. 1987. The psychological aspects of women with breast cancer. In I. M. Ariel and J. B. Cleary (eds.), *Breast cancer: Diagnosis and treatment* (531–536). New York: McGraw-Hill.

Spacks, P. 1985. *Gossip.* New York: Alfred A. Knopf.

Sparks, R. 1990. Skanks. *North American Review* 275(1):61–64.

Strasburger, V., and Brown, R. 1991. *Adolescent medicine: A practical guide.* Boston: Little, Brown.

Swallow, J. 1986. Both feet in life: Interviews with Barbara MacDonald and Cynthia Rich. In J. Alexander et al. (eds.), *Women and aging: An anthology by women* (193–203). Corvallis, Oreg.: Calyx Books.

Taylor, D., and Sumrall, A. C. (eds.) 1991. *Women of the 14th moon.* Freedom, Calif.: Crossing Press.

Taylor, R. C. 1992. Social differences in an elderly population. In J. G. Evans and R. F. Williams (eds.), *Oxford textbook of geriatric medicine.* Oxford: Oxford University Press.

The breast cancer digest. 1979. Bethesda: U.S. Department of Health, Education, and Welfare, Public Health Service, National Institutes of Heath (NIH Publication #80–1691).

Tillman, L. 1991. Critical fiction/critical self. In P. Mariani (ed.), *Critical fictions: The politics of imaginative writing. (97–103). Seattle: Bay Press.*

Tobey, S. B. 1991. *Art of motherhood.* New York: Abbeville Press.

Tong, R. 1989. *Feminist thought: A comprehensive introduction.* Boulder: Westview Press.

Townsend, R., and Perkins, A. (eds.). 1992. *Bitter fruit: Women's experiences of unplanned pregnancy, abortion, and adoption.* Alameda, Calif.: Hunter House.

Walker, A. 1991. Medicine. In *Her blue body everying we know: Earthling poems 1965–1990.* San Diego: Harcourt Brace Jovanovich.

———. 1981. The abortion. In *You can't keep a good woman down* (64–76). San Diego: Harcout Brace Jovanovich.

Willson, J. R. 1991a. Labor and delivery. In J. R. Willson and E. R. Carrington (eds.), *Obstetrics and gynecology,* 9th ed. (359–87). St. Louis: Mosby Year Book.

———. 1991b. Aging. In J. R. Willson and E. R. Carrington (eds.), *Obstetrics and gynecology,* 9th ed. (616–23). St. Louis: Mosby Year Book.

Wilson, M. D. 1990. Menstrual disorders. In R. A. Oski (ed.), *Principles and practice of pediatrics* (721–26). Philadelphia: Lippincott.

Wilt, J. 1992. Literature and maternal choice: From "instict" to conscious-ness. *Conscience: A newsjournal of prochoice Catholic opinion* 8(2):19–25.

Wittig, M. 1980. The straight mind. *Feminist Issues* 1(1):103–11.

Woodruff, M. 1987. Love at fifty. In S. Martz (ed.), *When I am an old woman I shall wear purple* (93). Watsonville, Calif.: Papier-Mache Press.

Woods, L. 1980. Conspiracy. In *MayDay! Quarterly.* Berkeley: Rainbow City Publications.

Zelman, Cynthia. 1991. Our menstruation. *Feminist Studies* 17(3):461–67.

Zuckerman, M. 1987. After sixty. In P. Doress and D. Seigel (eds.), *Our-selves, growing older* (405). New York: Simon and Schuster.

Index

V

W

Date Due